Challenges and Solutions in the Medical Field

C. P. Kumar
Reiki Healer
Roorkee - 247667, India

Copyright © 2023 C. P. Kumar

All rights reserved.

No part of this book may be reproduced or transmitted in any form or by any means, electronic or mechanical, including photocopying, recording, or by any information storage and retrieval system, without permission in writing from the author.

Disclaimer

While every effort has been made to ensure the accuracy and completeness of the content in this book, the author cannot guarantee that the information contained herein is error-free, up-to-date, or suitable for every individual circumstance.

The author shall not be held liable or responsible for any errors or omissions in the content of the book, nor for any damages, or losses that may arise from any actions taken based upon the suggestions or contents presented in the book.

Readers are advised to use their own judgment and discretion in applying the information provided in this book, and to consult with qualified professionals before taking any action based on the contents of this book. The author disclaims any and all liability or responsibility for any actions taken or not taken based on the information contained in this book.

DEDICATION

To all the dedicated healthcare professionals who tirelessly work to overcome the myriad challenges in the medical field, often in the face of adversity, uncertainty, and limited resources. Your unwavering commitment to the well-being of patients inspires us all.

To the patients and their families who navigate the complex healthcare landscape, enduring waiting times, disparities, and uncertainty, your resilience in the pursuit of health serves as a testament to the importance of our mission.

To the researchers, educators, and policymakers who strive to create a better future for healthcare, your innovation, knowledge, and dedication are instrumental in shaping the path forward.

May this book serve as a tribute to your efforts and an exploration of the challenges you face daily. Through understanding these challenges and proposing solutions, we hope to contribute to the betterment of healthcare for all. Together, let us envision a future where healthcare is accessible, equitable, efficient, and compassionate.

With profound respect,

C. P. Kumar

CONTENTS

PREFACE

In the intricate web of human existence, one facet stands out as indispensable - our health. Across epochs, across cultures, and throughout the annals of history, the pursuit of good health has remained a fundamental aspiration of humankind. The realm of medicine, with its ever-expanding boundaries, has been our ally in this quest, offering hope, healing, and solace in the face of ailments and adversities. Yet, for all the marvels of modern medicine, the path to preserving and enhancing our well-being is not without its obstacles.

Challenges and Solutions in the Medical Field seeks to illuminate the intricate tapestry of the healthcare landscape, where the pursuit of healing is juxtaposed with multifaceted hurdles. This book embarks on a journey through the intricate corridors of the medical field, traversing its many challenges and, importantly, charting out potential solutions.

The first chapter, *"Introduction to Medical Field Challenges,"* sets the stage for our exploration by underscoring the paramount importance of comprehending the obstacles that beset the world of medicine. It reminds us that to make strides toward a healthier world, we must first fathom the stumbling blocks on this arduous path.

In *"The Evolving Landscape of Medical Challenges,"* we delve deeper, recognizing that the medical terrain is not static but ever-evolving. Scientific advancements, technological integration, and shifting demographics usher in a new era of both possibilities and complexities, making it crucial to adapt and innovate.

This journey is not one that physicians and nurses tread alone. *"The Role of Nursing and Administration"* underscores the pivotal contribution of dedicated support staff in healthcare settings, without whom the wheels of healing would falter.

Healthcare is a dynamic field, one that pulsates with life, much like the heart it serves. *"Healthcare Workforce - Meeting Growing Demands"* discusses the mounting pressure on healthcare professionals, the struggles they face, and the imperative for ongoing education and training.

An alarming concern looms on the horizon: *"Shortage of Skilled Professionals"*. The scarcity of seasoned medical practitioners casts a shadow over the prospects of quality healthcare.

Global disparities in access to healthcare are laid bare in *"Access to Healthcare - A Global Concern"*. This chapter examines the pervasive healthcare inequality that persists across nations, raising questions of justice and ethics.

Differences between private and government healthcare systems are explored in *"Disparities in Healthcare"*. We scrutinize the contrasting realities of these two realms, shedding light on accessibility issues that persist.

"Inadequate Medical Infrastructure" takes us into the labyrinth of hospital facilities and equipment deficits. The very bedrock of medical care, these infrastructure gaps are, at times, a silent threat to patient well-being.

No facet of healthcare should be shrouded in neglect, including the most basic of needs. *"Sanitation and Hygiene Concerns"* confronts the grim reality of poor sanitation and hygiene in healthcare facilities, a stark paradox in the healing profession.

A battle is fought silently by countless patients who endure interminable waits in government hospitals. *"Patient Waiting Times"* unveils the poignant challenges they face, highlighting the urgent need for reforms.

But it is not just patients who suffer. *"Safety and Violence"* uncovers the shadow of fear that haunts medical professionals, illuminating instances of violence against those who dedicate their lives to healing.

Legal complexities entangle the healthcare landscape. *"Legal and Regulatory Frameworks"* navigates this intricate terrain, addressing issues of malpractice, liability, and the labyrinth of regulatory compliance.

The moral compass of medicine is dissected in *"Ethical Dilemmas"*. It grapples with the perplexing questions surrounding end-of-life care and the ethics of medical research.

The well-being of those who care for others cannot be overlooked. *"Mental Health and Well-being of Healthcare Workers"* explores the toll of burnout and stress, while also seeking out the support systems that can uplift those who heal.

In *"Public Health Crises"*, the crucible of the COVID-19 pandemic serves as a sobering reminder of the need for pandemic preparedness and equitable vaccine distribution, drawing lessons from a global crisis.

Balancing the books in healthcare is an art fraught with complexities. *"Healthcare Costs"* delves into the escalating financial burdens of healthcare, probing the delicate equilibrium between quality and affordability.

"*Private vs. Government Healthcare*" dissects the contrasting realms of healthcare delivery, shedding light on the unique challenges faced by each.

The unsettling phenomenon of "*Unnecessary Surgeries and Excessive Medical Testing*" is unmasked, revealing instances where medical care is compromised for financial gain, and highlighting the perils of overtreatment.

As our journey nears its end, "*Solutions and Recommendations*" offers a glimmer of hope. It proffers practical solutions and recommendations to confront the myriad challenges we have unearthed.

In our final chapter, "*Future of Healthcare*", we set our sights on the horizon, exploring potential advancements and changes that could usher in a brighter era for medicine, one where these challenges may be mitigated or overcome.

The pages that follow are a testament to our unwavering commitment to the ideals of healing and well-being. This book is a tribute to the tireless endeavors of those who dedicate their lives to the service of others and an invitation to all, beckoning us to join hands in surmounting the obstacles that lie ahead in the vast and ever-evolving landscape of the medical field.

C. P. Kumar
Reiki Healer
Former Scientist 'G', National Institute of Hydrology
Roorkee - 247667, India
E-mail: cpkumar@yahoo.com
Web: https://www.angelfire.com/nh/cpkumar/virgo.html

Chapter 1. Introduction to Medical Field Challenges

The field of medicine has long been regarded as one of the most noble and indispensable professions in society. It is a realm where dedicated professionals work tirelessly to alleviate human suffering, preserve life, and promote well-being. However, as noble as the profession may be, it is not without its formidable challenges. The complexities and intricacies of the modern healthcare system have given rise to a myriad of issues that demand our attention and concerted efforts to find solutions. In this introductory chapter, we will embark on a journey to explore and understand the challenges that permeate the medical field, emphasizing the crucial importance of recognizing and addressing these challenges.

The Evolving Landscape of Medical Challenges

The landscape of medicine is in a perpetual state of flux. Scientific advancements are a double-edged sword. On one hand, they have brought about groundbreaking treatments and life-saving innovations. On the other hand, the growing complexity of medical knowledge presents challenges in keeping healthcare professionals updated. Additionally, the integration of technology into healthcare, while promising efficiency, has raised concerns about data security and patient privacy.

Demographic changes, including an aging population and rising chronic diseases, have added to the complexity. The medical field must adapt to these evolving dynamics to provide effective care and maintain the delicate balance between tradition and innovation.

The Role of Nursing and Administration

While doctors often take center stage in healthcare, the role of nursing and administration cannot be overstated. Competent nurses are the backbone of patient care, providing critical support and often being the first point of contact for patients. Efficient administration ensures the smooth functioning of healthcare facilities. Understanding and addressing the unique challenges faced by nurses and administrators is paramount for a well-rounded healthcare system.

Healthcare Workforce

The demand for healthcare services is ever-increasing, leading to workforce shortages and burnout among medical professionals. The stress and exhaustion faced by healthcare workers can have detrimental effects on patient care. Adequate training and education are vital not only to address shortages but also to ensure that healthcare providers are equipped with the latest knowledge and skills.

Shortage of Skilled Professionals

The shortage of skilled medical professionals, particularly in specialized fields, poses a significant challenge. This shortage can lead to longer wait times, reduced access to care, and increased healthcare costs. Finding ways to attract and retain talented healthcare professionals is a critical issue in the medical field.

Access to Healthcare

Access to healthcare is a fundamental human right, yet it remains a global concern. Disparities in access to care, both within and between countries, persist. Addressing these disparities and striving for healthcare equality is essential to ensure that everyone, regardless of their background or location, has access to essential medical services.

Disparities in Healthcare

In many countries, healthcare systems consist of both private and government-run facilities. Analyzing the differences between these two systems is essential to understand disparities in healthcare. Accessibility issues, such as wait times and costs, can vary significantly between private and government healthcare, impacting patients' choices and outcomes.

Inadequate Medical Infrastructure

Inadequate medical infrastructure is a bottleneck in providing quality healthcare. Insufficient hospitals, clinics, and medical equipment can lead to suboptimal patient care. Addressing these infrastructure challenges is crucial to ensure that healthcare facilities are equipped to meet the needs of their communities.

Sanitation and Hygiene Concerns

Sanitation and hygiene are cornerstones of healthcare. Poor hygiene in healthcare facilities can lead to the spread of infections and compromise patient safety. This issue is particularly critical in preventing healthcare-associated infections and ensuring the well-being of patients and healthcare workers alike.

Patient Waiting Times

Long patient waiting times, especially in government hospitals, are a pervasive issue in many healthcare systems. Patients often endure extended wait times for consultations, diagnostics, and surgeries. This not only impacts patient satisfaction but can also lead to delays in diagnosis and treatment, potentially worsening health outcomes.

Safety and Violence

Healthcare professionals often face safety concerns and, tragically, incidents of violence. These issues compromise the safety and well-being of both patients and medical staff. Identifying strategies to enhance security within healthcare settings and address the root causes of violence is crucial for a safe and effective healthcare environment.

Legal and Regulatory Frameworks

The medical field operates within a complex web of legal and regulatory frameworks. Malpractice and liability concerns are ever-present, and healthcare providers must navigate these challenges while providing the best possible care. Understanding the legal landscape is essential to ensure ethical and responsible healthcare practices.

Ethical Dilemmas

Ethical dilemmas in healthcare are multifaceted. Choices regarding end-of-life care, organ transplantation, and research ethics require careful consideration of moral principles. These dilemmas can be emotionally taxing for healthcare professionals and patients alike, emphasizing the need for ethical guidance and decision-making frameworks.

Mental Health and Well-being of Healthcare Workers

The mental health and well-being of healthcare workers are under increasing strain. Burnout and stress are prevalent, affecting the quality of care provided. Establishing support systems and prioritizing the mental health of healthcare professionals is crucial to maintaining a resilient healthcare workforce.

Public Health Crises

The COVID-19 pandemic revealed the vulnerabilities in global healthcare systems. It emphasized the need for pandemic preparedness, effective vaccine distribution, and international collaboration in addressing public health crises. The lessons learned from this pandemic will shape future healthcare strategies and policies.

Healthcare Costs

Balancing healthcare quality and affordability is an ongoing challenge. Escalating healthcare costs can burden patients and strain healthcare budgets. Examining healthcare economics and exploring innovative cost-saving measures are vital to ensure that healthcare remains accessible without compromising quality.

Private vs. Government Healthcare

Private and government healthcare systems coexist in many countries, each with its advantages and challenges. Analyzing the differences between these systems helps policymakers make informed decisions and address disparities in healthcare access and quality.

Unnecessary Surgeries and Excessive Medical Testing

Instances of unnecessary surgeries and excessive medical testing raise ethical and financial concerns. Identifying and addressing these practices is essential to protect patients from harm and reduce healthcare costs.

Solutions and Recommendations

While the challenges in the medical field are formidable, they are not insurmountable. In this chapter, we will explore practical solutions and recommendations for addressing the complex issues discussed throughout the book. These solutions range from policy changes and healthcare system reforms to individual and community-level actions.

Future of Healthcare

The future of healthcare holds promise and potential for transformative advancements. In this final chapter, we will explore emerging technologies, innovative healthcare models, and potential changes in the medical field that could help alleviate some of the challenges discussed in this book. By embracing innovation and adapting to a rapidly evolving healthcare landscape, we can strive for a healthier and more equitable future for all.

Conclusion

The medical field is confronted with a multitude of challenges that have far-reaching implications for patient care, healthcare systems, and public health. These challenges are complex and multifaceted, requiring collaborative efforts from healthcare professionals, policymakers, researchers, and the community.

Understanding and addressing these challenges is not only necessary but also vital for the continued advancement of medicine and the well-being of individuals and society as a whole. By acknowledging these challenges and working towards innovative solutions, we can strive to create a healthcare system that is more equitable, efficient, and responsive to the needs of all patients.

Introduction

The field of medicine is in a constant state of evolution, driven by a multitude of factors that continually shape and reshape the landscape of healthcare. In this article, we will explore three pivotal aspects of this evolving medical landscape: scientific advancements and complexity, technological integration, and demographic changes. These factors intersect and interact, often presenting new challenges, but also offering innovative solutions that hold the promise of improving healthcare delivery and outcomes for all.

Scientific Advancements and Complexity

The relentless march of scientific progress has given rise to new medical challenges and opportunities. Here, we delve into the intricate web of scientific developments that both challenge and enrich modern healthcare.

1. Precision Medicine: Personalized Healthcare

One of the most exciting frontiers in modern medicine is the advent of precision medicine. This approach tailors medical treatment and interventions to individual patients based on their unique genetic makeup, environment, and lifestyle. While this promises better outcomes and fewer side effects, it also introduces the challenge of integrating vast datasets and making informed decisions about individualized treatment plans.

2. Genomic Medicine: Decoding the Human Genome

The mapping of the human genome has opened doors to a deeper understanding of genetic diseases and has paved the way for gene therapies. However, it has also given rise to ethical dilemmas surrounding genetic privacy and the potential for misuse of genetic information.

3. Infectious Diseases: A Shifting Battlefield

Infectious diseases, once thought to be on the decline, have resurged with the emergence of new pathogens, such as the SARS-CoV-2 virus responsible for COVID-19. Controlling these outbreaks demands not only scientific expertise but also effective public health measures and global cooperation.

4. Chronic Diseases: The Silent Epidemic

Non-communicable diseases like heart disease, diabetes, and cancer continue to pose a significant burden on healthcare systems worldwide. Managing these chronic conditions demands innovative approaches that extend beyond medical treatment to encompass lifestyle changes and preventive strategies.

Technological Integration

The integration of technology into healthcare has revolutionized the way medical services are delivered, but it has also introduced its own set of challenges.

1. Telemedicine

Telemedicine has emerged as a critical tool for increasing access to healthcare services, particularly in remote or underserved areas. However, it raises concerns about data security, the digital divide, and the need for standardized regulations.

2. Artificial Intelligence and Machine Learning

AI and machine learning are transforming diagnostics, treatment planning, and drug discovery. While they offer the potential to enhance medical decision-making, there are concerns about the transparency, accountability, and bias in algorithmic healthcare solutions.

3. Electronic Health Records (EHRs)

EHRs promise streamlined patient care and improved data sharing among healthcare providers. However, interoperability issues, data security breaches, and the administrative burden on healthcare professionals remain significant challenges.

4. Robotics in Surgery

Robotic-assisted surgery has brought unparalleled precision to the operating room. Still, it demands extensive training, high costs, and considerations about the potential over-reliance on technology.

Demographic Changes

The demographics of patients are changing, and healthcare systems must adapt to meet the unique needs of diverse populations.

1. Aging Population

As the world's population ages, healthcare systems must grapple with an increased demand for geriatric care, including managing chronic diseases, addressing mental health issues, and ensuring the elderly receive appropriate support and attention.

2. Healthcare Workforce

The healthcare workforce is facing increasing shortages in many regions, exacerbated by the aging population and the demands of the pandemic. Solutions to this challenge include expanding training programs, telehealth, and task-shifting strategies.

3. Health Disparities

Health disparities persist across different demographics, particularly among racial and ethnic groups. Addressing these disparities requires targeted interventions, increased cultural competency among healthcare providers, and equitable access to care.

4. Mental Health

The recognition of mental health as an integral part of overall well-being has grown, but access to mental healthcare remains a significant challenge. Strategies to address this issue include destigmatization, improved access to care, and integrating mental health services into primary care.

Conclusion

The landscape of medical challenges is ever-evolving, shaped by scientific advancements, technological integration, and demographic changes. While these factors introduce complexity and new obstacles to healthcare, they also present opportunities for innovation and progress. To navigate this evolving landscape successfully, healthcare stakeholders must work together to address the challenges and embrace the solutions that will define the future of medicine. As we continue to strive for better healthcare outcomes for all, it is imperative that we remain adaptable, ethically mindful, and patient-centered in our approach to these evolving challenges.

Introduction

The healthcare industry is a complex and dynamic field that requires a well-coordinated team effort to provide quality patient care. While doctors and nurses often take center stage in patient care, the role of competent support staff in healthcare settings cannot be understated. From administrative personnel to nursing assistants, these unsung heroes play a pivotal role in ensuring the smooth functioning of healthcare facilities. This article explores the significance of competent support staff in the medical field, shedding light on their multifaceted responsibilities, their impact on patient outcomes, and the challenges they face in their roles.

Administrative Support Staff

In any healthcare facility, administrative support staff form the backbone of day-to-day operations. Their responsibilities encompass a wide range of crucial tasks that enable healthcare providers to focus on patient care. These tasks include:

1. Patient Registration and Scheduling

Efficiently registering patients and scheduling appointments ensures that healthcare providers can manage their time effectively, reducing patient wait times and optimizing the use of resources.

2. Billing and Insurance Coordination

Accurate billing and insurance coordination are essential to the financial sustainability of healthcare organizations. Administrative staff must navigate complex insurance systems, submit claims, and assist patients in understanding their bills.

3. Medical Records Management

Maintaining accurate and up-to-date medical records is critical for continuity of care and ensuring patient safety. Administrative staff play a pivotal role in organizing, updating, and safeguarding patient records.

4. Compliance and Regulatory Requirements

Healthcare facilities must adhere to numerous regulatory standards and compliance measures. Administrative staff help ensure that the facility remains in compliance with all applicable laws and regulations.

5. Communication and Interdepartmental Coordination

Effective communication is key in healthcare settings. Administrative support staff facilitate communication between different departments, ensuring that information flows smoothly and that everyone is on the same page.

Nursing Assistants

Nursing assistants, also known as certified nursing assistants (CNAs) or patient care technicians (PCTs), are an integral part of the healthcare team. They work closely with registered nurses and licensed practical nurses to provide direct care to patients. Some of their key responsibilities include:

1. Patient Hygiene and Comfort

Nursing assistants assist with tasks such as bathing, dressing, and grooming, ensuring that patients maintain their hygiene and comfort.

2. Vital Signs Monitoring

Regular monitoring of vital signs, such as blood pressure, heart rate, and temperature, is crucial for assessing a patient's condition. Nursing assistants often take on this responsibility, allowing nurses to focus on more complex tasks.

3. Mobility and Rehabilitation Support

They help patients with mobility issues, ensuring that they can move safely and comfortably. They also assist in rehabilitation exercises prescribed by physical therapists.

4. Assisting with Activities of Daily Living (ADLs)

Nursing assistants help patients with activities they may struggle with due to illness or injury, including eating, toileting, and transferring.

5. Emotional Support

Providing emotional support to patients and their families is an essential aspect of the role. Compassion and empathy are key qualities that nursing assistants bring to their work.

The Impact of Competent Support Staff on Patient Outcomes

The presence of competent support staff in healthcare settings has a profound impact on patient outcomes and overall healthcare quality. Here's how their roles contribute to positive patient experiences.

1. Improved Efficiency and Workflow

Administrative support staff streamline administrative processes, reducing the time patients spend waiting for services. This efficiency leads to quicker access to care and better patient satisfaction.

2. Enhanced Safety and Patient Care

Nursing assistants help prevent complications by monitoring vital signs and addressing patients' basic needs promptly. This proactive approach can prevent deteriorations in patient conditions.

3. Reduced Nurse Workload

By taking on routine tasks, nursing assistants alleviate some of the workload on registered nurses. This allows nurses to focus on tasks that require their specialized skills, leading to better overall patient care.

4. Personalized Patient Care

Support staff, including administrative personnel, play a critical role in ensuring that patients receive personalized care. They help gather and manage patient information, ensuring that healthcare providers have the necessary data to make informed decisions.

5. Positive Patient Experience

A well-coordinated team that includes competent support staff can contribute to a positive patient experience. Patients who feel well-cared for and supported during their healthcare journey are more likely to have better outcomes and satisfaction.

Challenges Faced by Support Staff in Healthcare

Despite their invaluable contributions, support staff in healthcare settings often face unique challenges that can affect their job satisfaction and performance. Some of these challenges include:

1. Heavy Workload

Administrative support staff may have to juggle multiple tasks simultaneously, leading to a heavy workload. This can be stressful and affect their ability to provide quality service.

2. Emotional Toll

Nursing assistants often witness patients in vulnerable and distressing situations. Providing emotional support can take an emotional toll on these caregivers.

3. Lack of Recognition

Support staff's contributions are sometimes overlooked or undervalued in healthcare settings. They may not receive the recognition and appreciation they deserve.

4. Limited Advancement Opportunities

In some cases, support staff may face limited opportunities for career advancement or professional development, which can impact their job satisfaction and motivation.

5. Exposure to Health Risks

Nursing assistants and other frontline support staff may be at risk of exposure to infectious diseases, which adds an element of physical risk to their roles.

Strategies for Supporting and Empowering Healthcare Support Staff

Recognizing the importance of competent support staff in healthcare, it is crucial to implement strategies that support and empower them in their roles.

1. Training and Education

Providing ongoing training and education opportunities for support staff can enhance their skills and knowledge, allowing them to perform their roles more effectively.

2. Recognition and Appreciation

Regularly acknowledging and appreciating the contributions of support staff can boost morale and job satisfaction. Small gestures of recognition can go a long way.

3. Career Pathways

Creating clear career pathways and advancement opportunities for support staff can motivate them to excel in their roles and invest in their long-term careers in healthcare.

4. Employee Assistance Programs (EAPs)

EAPs can offer support to staff dealing with the emotional toll of their roles, providing resources for counseling and mental health support.

5. Workplace Safety Measures

Ensuring the safety of support staff, especially those in direct patient care roles, is essential. Adequate personal protective equipment (PPE) and infection control measures must be in place.

Conclusion

The healthcare industry relies on a well-coordinated team of professionals to deliver quality care to patients. While doctors and nurses are often in the spotlight, competent support staff in healthcare settings are the unsung heroes who work tirelessly behind the scenes. Administrative support staff ensure that operations run smoothly, while nursing assistants provide direct care and support to patients. Their combined efforts have a significant impact on patient outcomes, efficiency, and overall healthcare quality.

Recognizing the challenges faced by support staff and implementing strategies to support and empower them is essential for maintaining a robust healthcare system. By valuing and investing in the contributions of these dedicated individuals, we can ensure that healthcare facilities continue to provide exceptional care and support to patients, ultimately improving the well-being of communities worldwide.

Introduction

The healthcare industry is at a crossroads, facing unprecedented challenges and opportunities. As the demand for healthcare services continues to surge due to aging populations, emerging health crises, and technological advancements, the pressure on the healthcare workforce is reaching critical levels. This article explores the multifaceted challenges of shortages and burnout in the healthcare workforce and examines the vital role of training and education in addressing these issues.

Shortages in the Healthcare Workforce

1. Demographic Shifts

The first challenge to address is the shortage of healthcare professionals, particularly in high-demand fields such as nursing, primary care, and mental health services. One of the key drivers of this shortage is demographic shifts. As the global population ages, the demand for healthcare services has never been higher. This demographic trend places significant strain on healthcare providers, as they struggle to meet the needs of an increasingly elderly population with complex healthcare requirements.

2. Specialty Shortages

In addition to the general shortage of healthcare workers, there is a shortage of specialists in certain regions and healthcare facilities. This is often exacerbated by maldistribution, where healthcare professionals tend to cluster in urban areas, leaving rural and underserved communities with limited access to essential medical services. This maldistribution highlights the need for innovative solutions to attract and retain healthcare professionals in underserved areas.

3. Pandemic Impact

The COVID-19 pandemic exposed the vulnerabilities of healthcare systems worldwide. Healthcare workers were stretched to their limits, working long hours and facing unprecedented stress. Many experienced burnout and exhaustion, leading some to leave the profession altogether. While the pandemic has accelerated the adoption of telemedicine and digital health solutions, it has also highlighted the need for a resilient healthcare workforce that can respond effectively to crises.

Burnout Among Healthcare Professionals

1. Definition and Impact

Burnout among healthcare professionals is a pervasive problem that has far-reaching consequences. It is characterized by emotional exhaustion, depersonalization, and a reduced sense of personal accomplishment. The demanding nature of healthcare work, combined with long hours and high-stress environments, makes healthcare professionals particularly vulnerable to burnout.

The impact of burnout is felt not only by healthcare workers themselves but also by patients and the healthcare system as a whole. Burnout can lead to decreased job performance, medical errors, increased turnover, and decreased patient satisfaction. In essence, the healthcare workforce's burnout crisis threatens the quality and safety of patient care.

2. Causes of Burnout

Several factors contribute to burnout among healthcare professionals.

Workload: Heavy workloads, including long hours and an increased patient-to-provider ratio, leave healthcare workers physically and emotionally drained.

Emotional Stress: Healthcare workers frequently encounter emotionally charged situations, such as patient suffering and loss. This emotional burden takes a toll over time.

Administrative Tasks: The administrative burden placed on healthcare professionals, including documentation and regulatory requirements, often diverts their attention from patient care.

Lack of Resources: Insufficient resources, including staffing shortages and inadequate equipment, can make it challenging to deliver high-quality care and contribute to burnout.

3. Mitigating Burnout

Addressing burnout in the healthcare workforce requires a multifaceted approach.

Supportive Work Environments: Healthcare organizations must foster supportive and empathetic work environments that prioritize the well-being of their employees.

Workload Management: Implementing measures to manage workloads, such as appropriate staffing levels and efficient administrative processes, can alleviate some of the stressors that contribute to burnout.

Mental Health Resources: Providing access to mental health resources and support services can help healthcare professionals cope with the emotional toll of their work.

Training in Resilience: Healthcare workers should be trained in resilience and stress management techniques to better navigate the challenges they face.

Training and Education

1. The Role of Education

Training and education are pivotal in addressing both the shortage and burnout challenges in the healthcare workforce. Educational institutions and healthcare organizations must collaborate to produce well-prepared, resilient, and adaptable healthcare professionals.

Holistic Education: Healthcare education should not only focus on technical skills but also emphasize the importance of empathy, communication, and cultural competence. These skills are essential for providing patient-centered care.

Interdisciplinary Training: Encouraging interdisciplinary collaboration and training can improve healthcare delivery by fostering a deeper understanding of different roles and perspectives within the healthcare team.

Lifelong Learning: Healthcare professionals should be encouraged to engage in lifelong learning and professional development to stay updated on the latest medical advances and best practices.

2. Addressing Workforce Shortages

Expansion of Training Programs: To address shortages in high-demand fields, educational institutions should expand their training programs and increase enrollment in nursing, primary care, and mental health specialties.

Scholarships and Incentives: Offering scholarships, loan forgiveness programs, and financial incentives can attract individuals to underserved areas and fields with workforce shortages.

Telemedicine Training: With the rise of telemedicine, healthcare professionals should receive training in remote care delivery to expand access to healthcare services in rural and remote areas.

3. Combating Burnout Through Education

Emotional Intelligence Training: Healthcare education should incorporate emotional intelligence training to help future professionals cope with the emotional challenges of patient care.

Resilience Training: Teaching resilience skills can better prepare healthcare workers to manage stress and prevent burnout.

Interprofessional Education: Collaborative training programs that bring together healthcare professionals from different disciplines can enhance teamwork, communication, and mutual support.

Conclusion

The healthcare workforce is facing unprecedented challenges, with shortages and burnout threatening the quality of patient care. Addressing these issues requires a concerted effort from educational institutions, healthcare organizations, policymakers, and healthcare professionals themselves.

By investing in comprehensive education that emphasizes empathy, communication, and resilience, we can prepare a workforce that is not only clinically competent but also better equipped to navigate the emotional demands of healthcare. Additionally, innovative strategies such as expanding training programs, offering incentives, and embracing telemedicine can help alleviate workforce shortages in critical areas.

The healthcare workforce is the backbone of our healthcare system, and its well-being and preparedness are essential for ensuring the health and well-being of our communities. It is imperative that we prioritize the training and education of healthcare professionals to meet the growing demands of the future while safeguarding their own physical and emotional well-being. Only through these efforts can we build a stronger and more resilient healthcare workforce capable of delivering high-quality care to all.

Introduction

The healthcare industry is a cornerstone of modern society, providing essential services that save lives and improve the quality of life for millions of people worldwide. However, the healthcare sector faces a significant challenge – a shortage of skilled professionals, particularly experienced medical professionals. This issue not only affects the quality of care patients receive but also has broader implications for healthcare systems, economies, and public health. In this article, we will delve into the root causes of the shortage, its impact on healthcare delivery, and potential solutions to address this critical issue.

Understanding the Shortage

1. The Demographic Shift

One of the primary reasons behind the shortage of experienced medical professionals is the demographic shift occurring in many developed countries. As the baby boomer generation (people born from 1946 to 1964) retires, the demand for healthcare services is rising due to the aging population. This creates a double-edged sword, as both patients and the healthcare workforce are aging simultaneously.

Retirement Wave: A significant portion of the medical workforce is nearing retirement age, leading to a wave of experienced professionals leaving the workforce.

Growing Demand: As the elderly population increases, there is a growing demand for healthcare services, particularly for specialized care and chronic disease management.

2. Educational Barriers

Becoming a medical professional requires years of education, including undergraduate studies, medical school, internships, and residencies. These rigorous educational requirements can deter potential candidates from pursuing careers in medicine.

Lengthy Education: **Medical education is time-consuming, with the entire process taking over a decade, which can discourage individuals from pursuing medical careers.**

Financial Burden: **The cost of medical education can be exorbitant, leading to significant student loan debt for those who do choose this path.**

3. Specialty Shortages

The shortage of skilled professionals is not evenly distributed across all medical specialties. Some areas, such as primary care and certain subspecialties, are more affected than others.

Primary Care Shortage: **Many regions face a shortage of primary care physicians, who play a crucial role in preventive care and early diagnosis.**

Subspecialty Gaps: **Highly specialized fields like oncology and neurosurgery often experience shortages, leading to long waiting times for patients in need.**

Impact on Healthcare Delivery

1. Longer Wait Times

One of the most immediate consequences of the shortage of experienced medical professionals is longer wait times for patients seeking care. This can lead to delayed diagnoses, treatment, and increased suffering.

Delayed Diagnoses: Longer wait times can result in delays in diagnosing conditions, which can impact treatment outcomes.

Treatment Delays: Patients may face delays in receiving necessary treatments, leading to worsening health conditions.

2. Overworked Staff

Healthcare professionals are often overworked due to understaffing. This can have detrimental effects on both the professionals themselves and the quality of care they provide.

Burnout: Overworked medical professionals are at a higher risk of burnout, which can lead to decreased job satisfaction and even early retirement.

Increased Errors: Fatigue and stress can lead to medical errors, compromising patient safety.

3. Unequal Access

The shortage of experienced medical professionals can exacerbate existing healthcare disparities, as underserved communities often bear the brunt of this issue.

Rural Healthcare: **Rural areas are particularly affected, with** limited access to healthcare services due to a lack of medical professionals.

Socioeconomic Disparities: **Low-income communities** often struggle to attract experienced medical professionals, leading to unequal access to quality care.

Potential Solutions

Addressing the shortage of skilled medical professionals requires a multi-pronged approach involving changes in education, healthcare delivery, and policy.

1. Expanding Medical Education

To increase the pool of qualified medical professionals, efforts should be made to expand medical education programs.

Streamlining Education: **Exploring ways to shorten the** duration of medical education without compromising quality can make the path to becoming a medical professional more accessible.

Scholarships and Financial Aid: **Offering more scholarships** and financial aid programs can help alleviate the financial burden of medical education.

2. Telemedicine and Technology

Leveraging technology, such as telemedicine and AI-assisted diagnosis, can help bridge the gap between patient demand and medical supply.

Telemedicine: Telemedicine is the remote provision of healthcare services and consultations using telecommunications technology. Expanding telemedicine services can provide patients with access to healthcare professionals regardless of geographical constraints.

AI and Automation: AI can assist healthcare professionals in tasks like diagnostics and administrative work, increasing efficiency. AI-assisted diagnosis refers to the use of artificial intelligence and machine learning algorithms to aid healthcare professionals in diagnosing medical conditions, interpreting medical images, and analyzing patient data for more accurate and efficient diagnoses.

3. Workforce Diversity

Promoting diversity in the healthcare workforce can help address disparities in care and attract a broader range of individuals to the field.

Diversity Initiatives: Implementing diversity initiatives in medical schools and healthcare organizations can create a more inclusive environment.

Outreach Programs: Encouraging underrepresented minorities to pursue medical careers through outreach programs and mentorship can help diversify the workforce.

4. Incentives and Benefits

Offering incentives and improved benefits can make the medical profession more attractive, retaining experienced professionals and attracting new talent.

Loan Forgiveness Programs: Implementing loan forgiveness programs for medical professionals who commit to working in underserved areas can encourage recruitment.

Competitive Salaries: Offering competitive salaries and benefits can reduce turnover rates among healthcare professionals.

5. International Collaboration

Collaboration on a global scale can help alleviate shortages by sharing knowledge, expertise, and resources.

International Recruitment: Encouraging international medical professionals to work in regions with shortages can be part of the solution.

Knowledge Sharing: Facilitating the exchange of medical knowledge and best practices among countries can improve healthcare delivery.

Conclusion

The shortage of skilled medical professionals, particularly experienced ones, is a pressing challenge that healthcare systems worldwide must confront. As the demand for healthcare services continues to rise due to an aging population, addressing this issue is imperative. By expanding medical education, leveraging technology, promoting diversity, offering incentives, and fostering international collaboration, we can work towards a healthcare system that ensures equal access to quality care for all. The path ahead may be challenging, but the health and well-being of our communities depend on our ability to overcome this shortage and build a sustainable future for the medical profession.

Chapter 6. Access to Healthcare
A Global Concern

Introduction

Access to healthcare is a fundamental human right, a cornerstone of social justice, and a critical determinant of overall well-being. However, despite significant advancements in medical science and healthcare infrastructure worldwide, disparities in access to healthcare persist as a global concern. This article explores the multifaceted issue of healthcare inequality, shedding light on the root causes, consequences, and potential solutions to bridge the gap in healthcare access. From socioeconomic disparities to geographical limitations, healthcare inequality takes various forms, affecting individuals and communities in both developed and developing nations.

Understanding Healthcare Inequality

1. Socioeconomic Disparities in Access

One of the most prominent and pervasive forms of healthcare inequality revolves around socioeconomic factors. Income, education, and employment play pivotal roles in determining one's access to quality healthcare. Low-income individuals and families often face barriers such as limited health insurance coverage, high out-of-pocket costs, and a lack of resources to access preventive care. This disparity in access contributes to delayed diagnoses and poorer health outcomes among marginalized populations.

2. Geographical Limitations

Access to healthcare is also greatly influenced by geographic factors. Rural and remote areas frequently lack the healthcare infrastructure found in urban centers. Patients in these regions often struggle with longer travel times to reach medical facilities, limited access to specialized care, and shortages of healthcare providers. Geographic disparities not only affect individual patients but also impact the overall health status of communities in underserved areas.

3. Racial and Ethnic Disparities

Healthcare inequality is further compounded by racial and ethnic disparities. Minority populations often face systemic barriers that hinder their access to quality healthcare. These barriers can include discrimination, cultural insensitivity, and language barriers. Consequently, minority communities experience disparities in health outcomes, including higher rates of chronic diseases and lower life expectancy.

4. Gender-Based Inequalities

Gender-based healthcare disparities are another facet of this complex issue. Women, for instance, often encounter obstacles in accessing reproductive healthcare, including contraception and maternal care. Gender inequality extends to research and clinical trials, where women are historically underrepresented, leading to gaps in understanding the unique healthcare needs of women.

5. Inadequate Health Infrastructure

In many regions, healthcare infrastructure remains underdeveloped and underfunded. This leads to shortages of essential medical facilities, equipment, and healthcare professionals. Insufficient infrastructure not only limits access to healthcare but also compromises the quality of care available. Moreover, weak healthcare systems are ill-equipped to respond effectively to public health crises, as highlighted by the COVID-19 pandemic.

The Consequences of Healthcare Inequality

1. Health Disparities

The consequences of healthcare inequality are far-reaching, impacting individuals and communities in profound ways. Health disparities, driven by unequal access to healthcare, result in variations in health outcomes among different population groups. These disparities are particularly evident in higher rates of chronic diseases, reduced life expectancy, and poorer overall health in marginalized communities.

2. Economic Burden

Healthcare inequality places a significant economic burden on society. When individuals lack access to preventive care and timely medical interventions, they often seek healthcare services at more advanced disease stages, which are costlier to treat. This increased healthcare expenditure strains both public and private healthcare systems, diverting resources away from prevention and early intervention.

3. Social Inequity

Healthcare inequality reinforces broader social inequities. The inability to access healthcare perpetuates cycles of poverty and disadvantage, limiting opportunities for personal and economic advancement. Inequitable healthcare systems can erode trust in institutions and exacerbate social divisions, further deepening disparities in access.

Addressing Healthcare Inequality

1. Universal Healthcare Coverage

One of the most effective ways to address healthcare inequality is through the establishment of universal healthcare coverage. This approach ensures that every citizen has access to essential healthcare services regardless of their socioeconomic status, location, or other demographic factors. Several countries have successfully implemented universal healthcare systems, which have led to improved health outcomes and reduced healthcare disparities.

2. Investment in Healthcare Infrastructure

Investing in healthcare infrastructure is essential for improving access to healthcare services, particularly in underserved areas. Governments and international organizations should prioritize building and maintaining healthcare facilities, ensuring the availability of medical equipment, and incentivizing healthcare professionals to work in underserved regions.

3. Healthcare Workforce Development

Strengthening the healthcare workforce is critical for reducing disparities in access. This involves increasing the number of healthcare professionals, particularly in areas with shortages, and providing training and education programs to enhance the skills of existing healthcare workers. Additionally, efforts should be made to diversify the healthcare workforce to better serve the needs of diverse patient populations.

4. Reducing Socioeconomic Barriers

Addressing socioeconomic disparities in access to healthcare requires a multifaceted approach. This includes implementing policies to reduce out-of-pocket costs for low-income individuals, expanding Medicaid and other safety-net programs, and improving access to affordable health insurance. Incentives for employers to provide comprehensive health benefits can also play a role in reducing healthcare inequality.

5. Cultural Competence and Anti-Discrimination Measures

To combat racial, ethnic, and gender-based disparities, healthcare systems must prioritize cultural competence training for healthcare providers. Additionally, anti-discrimination measures should be enforced to ensure that all patients receive equitable treatment, regardless of their background or identity. This includes addressing implicit biases within the healthcare system.

6. Health Education and Promotion

Promoting health literacy and education is crucial for empowering individuals to take control of their health. Public health campaigns and educational initiatives can raise awareness about preventive measures, healthy lifestyles, and the importance of early intervention. By equipping individuals with knowledge, healthcare systems can reduce the burden of preventable diseases.

7. Global Collaboration

Healthcare inequality is not confined to individual countries but is a global concern. International collaboration is essential to address disparities in access to healthcare on a global scale. This includes sharing best practices, pooling resources, and providing support to developing nations to strengthen their healthcare systems.

Conclusion

Access to healthcare is a fundamental right that should be available to all, regardless of their background or circumstances. Healthcare inequality, driven by socioeconomic, geographic, racial, ethnic, and gender-based disparities, has profound consequences for individuals and society as a whole. Addressing these disparities requires a comprehensive and multifaceted approach, including universal healthcare coverage, investment in healthcare infrastructure, workforce development, and measures to reduce socioeconomic and cultural barriers. By working together on a global scale, we can strive to eliminate healthcare inequality and ensure that everyone has the opportunity to achieve their highest attainable standard of health.

Introduction

Access to quality healthcare is a fundamental right that every individual should enjoy, irrespective of their socio-economic status or geographic location. Unfortunately, disparities in healthcare continue to persist, and these disparities are often shaped by the type of healthcare system in place. This article delves into the critical issue of healthcare disparities, focusing on the differences between private and government healthcare systems and the accessibility issues associated with them. By exploring these disparities, we can gain a better understanding of the challenges and potential solutions within the medical field.

Private vs. Government Healthcare Systems

1. Private Healthcare Systems

Private healthcare systems, characterized by their reliance on privately-owned hospitals, clinics, and insurance providers, are widely prevalent in many countries. These systems offer certain advantages, including shorter wait times, a broader range of services, and access to state-of-the-art medical technologies. However, they come with their own set of challenges.

Cost Barriers: One of the most significant disparities in private healthcare is the cost barrier. High premiums, deductibles, and out-of-pocket expenses can make private healthcare inaccessible for many individuals and families, particularly those with lower incomes. This financial burden can lead to delayed or avoided medical care, ultimately impacting health outcomes.

Uneven Distribution: Private healthcare providers tend to be concentrated in urban areas, leaving rural populations with limited access. This geographical disparity can result in delayed diagnoses, limited preventative care, and reduced health outcomes for those living in remote regions.

Profit Motive: Private healthcare providers are driven by profit, which can sometimes lead to overuse of medical services, unnecessary tests, and treatments. This overutilization can increase healthcare costs for both patients and insurers, contributing to the overall healthcare expenditure.

2. Government Healthcare Systems

Government healthcare systems, often referred to as universal healthcare or single-payer systems, aim to provide equitable healthcare services to all citizens. While these systems eliminate many of the cost barriers associated with private healthcare, they also face their own set of challenges:

Funding and Resource Allocation: Government healthcare systems rely on public funding, which can be limited. This can lead to resource constraints, including longer wait times for certain medical procedures and limitations on access to specialized care.

Bureaucracy and Red Tape: The administration of government healthcare systems can be burdened by bureaucracy and red tape, which can slow down decision-making and hinder timely access to care.

Limited Choice: In some government healthcare systems, patients may have limited choice when it comes to their healthcare providers and treatments. This lack of choice can lead to dissatisfaction and reduced patient engagement in their healthcare.

Healthcare Disparities and Vulnerable Populations

1. Racial and Ethnic Disparities

Healthcare disparities often intersect with race and ethnicity, leading to significant inequities in access to care and health outcomes. Minority populations, particularly Black, Indigenous, and People of Color (BIPOC), often face higher rates of chronic illnesses, reduced access to preventative care, and increased mortality rates compared to their white counterparts. These disparities are rooted in historical injustices, systemic racism, and socio-economic factors.

2. Socioeconomic Disparities

Socioeconomic status plays a pivotal role in healthcare disparities. Individuals with lower incomes may struggle to afford private healthcare or face barriers in accessing government healthcare due to limited resources and transportation issues. These disparities can result in delayed diagnoses, untreated conditions, and poorer health outcomes among economically disadvantaged populations.

3. Geographic Disparities

Access to healthcare services can vary significantly based on geographic location. Rural communities often have limited access to healthcare facilities, specialists, and emergency services. This geographical divide can result in delayed treatment, especially for conditions requiring immediate attention, such as heart attacks or strokes.

Addressing Healthcare Disparities

1. Improving Healthcare Access

Expanding Insurance Coverage: Expanding access to health insurance, either through government programs or private options, can reduce financial barriers to healthcare.

Telemedicine: Leveraging telemedicine can bridge the gap in healthcare access for individuals in remote areas. It provides a cost-effective means of receiving medical consultations and monitoring chronic conditions.

Community Health Centers: Investing in community health centers can enhance access to primary care for underserved populations, particularly in rural areas.

2. Enhancing Preventative Care

Health Education: Promoting health education programs can empower individuals to take proactive steps in managing their health and preventing illnesses.

Early Detection and Screening: Ensuring regular screenings and early detection programs for diseases like cancer can significantly improve outcomes.

3. Addressing Socioeconomic Disparities

Income Support: Implementing income support programs can alleviate the financial burden on low-income individuals and families, enabling them to access necessary healthcare.

Affordable Medications: Initiatives to reduce the cost of prescription medications can make healthcare more affordable for all.

Housing and Food Security: Addressing social determinants of health, such as housing and food security, can improve overall health outcomes for vulnerable populations.

Reducing Racial and Ethnic Disparities

Anti-Racist Policies: Implementing anti-racist policies within healthcare systems and institutions can address systemic racism and reduce disparities.

Culturally Competent Care: Training healthcare providers to deliver culturally competent care can improve patient trust and engagement.

Data Collection and Research: Collecting comprehensive data on healthcare disparities and conducting research to understand their root causes is essential for developing effective interventions.

Conclusion

Disparities in healthcare persist in both private and government healthcare systems, with varying challenges associated with each. While private healthcare systems can pose financial barriers and geographical disparities, government healthcare systems may face resource constraints and bureaucratic challenges. Addressing these disparities requires a multifaceted approach that includes expanding access to healthcare, enhancing preventative care, addressing socioeconomic disparities, and reducing racial and ethnic disparities.

To truly overcome healthcare disparities, it is essential to view healthcare as a human right and work collectively to ensure that all individuals, regardless of their background or circumstances, have equitable access to quality healthcare services. This commitment to equity in healthcare will not only improve individual health outcomes but also contribute to a healthier and more just society for all. As we continue to face challenges in the medical field, addressing healthcare disparities must remain a top priority to achieve the goal of accessible and high-quality healthcare for everyone.

Introduction

The foundation of any effective healthcare system lies in its medical infrastructure. Hospitals, clinics, and medical equipment serve as the backbone of healthcare delivery, ensuring that individuals receive timely and quality medical care. However, inadequate medical infrastructure can hinder the healthcare system's ability to meet the needs of its population. In this article, we will delve into the various issues related to hospitals, clinics, and medical equipment, shedding light on the challenges they pose to healthcare systems around the world. Additionally, we will explore potential solutions to address these pressing problems.

Underfunded and Overcrowded Hospitals

One of the most glaring issues in medical infrastructure is the chronic underfunding and overcrowding of hospitals. These problems often go hand in hand, exacerbating each other's negative impact on patient care.

1. Lack of Adequate Funding

Hospitals require substantial financial resources to provide high-quality care. Unfortunately, many healthcare facilities, especially in developing countries, face chronic underfunding. This lack of funding can result in inadequate staffing, outdated equipment, and poorly maintained facilities, all of which can compromise patient safety and the quality of care.

2. Overcrowding

Overcrowded hospitals are a common sight in many parts of the world. This overcrowding can lead to extended waiting times, overworked healthcare staff, and a decreased quality of care. Patients may have to share beds, and critical cases might be delayed due to the sheer volume of patients seeking treatment.

Solutions

Increase Funding: Governments and healthcare authorities must allocate more resources to hospitals. This includes increased budgets for personnel, facility maintenance, and equipment upgrades.

Build Additional Capacity: Investing in the construction of new healthcare facilities or expanding existing ones can help alleviate overcrowding. This should be done strategically to ensure equitable access to healthcare.

Insufficient Clinics in Rural Areas

Access to healthcare is a fundamental right, yet millions of people in rural areas face significant challenges in accessing even basic medical services due to a lack of clinics.

1. Geographical Barriers

Rural areas are often geographically isolated, making it difficult for residents to reach healthcare facilities. The absence of clinics in these areas can lead to delayed diagnoses, untreated conditions, and preventable health complications.

2. Shortage of Healthcare Professionals

Even when clinics exist in rural areas, they often suffer from a shortage of healthcare professionals. Doctors, nurses, and other healthcare workers are more likely to be concentrated in urban centers, leaving rural clinics understaffed and overwhelmed.

Solutions

Telemedicine and Mobile Clinics: Telemedicine is the remote provision of healthcare services and consultations using telecommunications technology. Mobile clinics are movable healthcare facilities that provide medical services to underserved or remote areas. Leveraging telemedicine and mobile clinics can help bridge the gap between rural communities and healthcare services. Telehealth allows patients to consult with doctors remotely, while mobile clinics can provide on-site care in underserved areas.

Incentivize Rural Healthcare: Governments can provide incentives, such as scholarships and loan forgiveness programs, to encourage healthcare professionals to work in rural areas.

Aging and Inadequate Medical Equipment

The effective diagnosis and treatment of medical conditions heavily depend on the availability of modern and well-maintained medical equipment. Unfortunately, many healthcare facilities grapple with aging and inadequate equipment.

1. Outdated Technology

Outdated medical equipment can hinder accurate diagnoses and treatment. For instance, older imaging machines may produce lower-quality images, making it difficult for healthcare providers to detect and treat conditions effectively.

2. Lack of Maintenance

Even when healthcare facilities have modern equipment, the lack of regular maintenance can lead to breakdowns and reduced reliability. This can disrupt patient care and result in costly repairs.

Solutions

Equipment Upgrade Programs: Implementing equipment upgrade programs on a regular basis ensures that healthcare facilities have access to modern technology. These programs can be funded through public-private partnerships or government initiatives.

Preventive Maintenance: Establishing robust preventive maintenance schedules for medical equipment can extend their lifespan and ensure they remain in good working condition.

Inadequate Disaster Preparedness

Natural disasters and public health emergencies can strain healthcare infrastructure to its limits. Inadequate disaster preparedness can lead to chaos and endanger both patients and healthcare workers.

1. Lack of Emergency Response Plans

Hospitals and clinics must have comprehensive emergency response plans in place. Without these plans, healthcare facilities may struggle to respond effectively to disasters such as hurricanes, earthquakes, or pandemics.

2. Insufficient Supplies and Resources

Disasters can quickly deplete medical supplies and resources. Inadequate stockpiles of essential items like personal protective equipment (PPE), ventilators, and medications can jeopardize patient care during emergencies.

Solutions

Develop and Test Emergency Plans: Healthcare facilities should create and regularly test emergency response plans to ensure they are prepared for various types of disasters.

Stockpile Essential Supplies: Maintaining an adequate stockpile of critical supplies and resources is essential for responding to emergencies. Collaboration with government agencies can help facilitate this.

Inequities in Access to Specialized Care

Access to specialized medical care is often unevenly distributed, with urban areas enjoying more comprehensive services than rural and underserved regions.

1. Urban-Centric Care

Specialized medical services, such as organ transplantation, cancer treatment centers, and advanced surgical procedures, are often concentrated in urban areas. This concentration can create significant disparities in healthcare access.

2. Geographic and Socioeconomic Barriers

Geographic and socioeconomic barriers further exacerbate the inequities in access to specialized care. Patients from remote or disadvantaged areas may face prohibitive costs and logistical challenges in seeking specialized treatment.

Solutions

Regional Healthcare Networks: Establishing regional healthcare networks can ensure that specialized care is accessible to a broader population. These networks can facilitate the transfer of patients between facilities.

Telemedicine for Consultations: Telemedicine can be used to connect patients in remote areas with specialist doctors located in urban centers, reducing the need for extensive travel.

Conclusion

Inadequate medical infrastructure poses significant challenges to the healthcare system, affecting the quality, accessibility, and equity of care. Addressing these issues requires a multi-faceted approach, including increased funding, strategic planning, and the use of technology to bridge gaps in healthcare delivery. By recognizing and tackling these problems head-on, we can work towards building a more resilient and inclusive healthcare system that meets the diverse needs of our populations, regardless of location or socioeconomic status.

Chapter 9. Sanitation and Hygiene Concerns

Introduction

Healthcare facilities are places of healing, places where patients come to receive treatment and care. They are meant to be sanctuaries of health and well-being, where diseases are diagnosed and treated, and lives are saved. However, for all the life-saving work that takes place within their walls, healthcare facilities around the world often face a critical challenge – poor sanitation and hygiene. This issue poses a grave threat to both patients and healthcare workers, undermining the very purpose of these institutions. In this article, we will delve into the various facets of this issue, exploring its causes, consequences, and possible solutions, all within the context of the book "Challenges and Solutions in the Medical Field."

The Importance of Sanitation and Hygiene in Healthcare Facilities

1. The Role of Sanitation in Infection Control

Sanitation and hygiene are integral to the prevention and control of infections within healthcare facilities. Proper sanitation measures, including regular cleaning and disinfection, help eliminate pathogens that can lead to healthcare-associated infections (HAIs). HAIs are a significant concern, as they can prolong hospital stays, increase healthcare costs, and, in severe cases, lead to patient mortality.

2. Hygiene Practices for Healthcare Workers

Healthcare workers play a crucial role in maintaining a safe and sterile environment within healthcare facilities. Adhering to stringent hygiene practices, such as handwashing, wearing personal protective equipment (PPE), and following aseptic techniques, is essential for minimizing the risk of cross-contamination between patients and the spread of infectious diseases.

Causes of Poor Sanitation and Hygiene in Healthcare Facilities

1. Resource Constraints

One of the primary reasons for inadequate sanitation and hygiene in healthcare facilities is resource constraints. Many healthcare institutions, particularly those in low-income regions, struggle with limited budgets, insufficient staff, and inadequate infrastructure. This lack of resources can result in compromised sanitation and hygiene standards.

2. Inadequate Training and Awareness

In some cases, healthcare workers may not receive adequate training on proper sanitation and hygiene practices. This can lead to gaps in knowledge and suboptimal compliance with infection control protocols. Furthermore, the importance of these practices may not be adequately emphasized or communicated to staff.

3. Overcrowding and High Patient Loads

Overcrowding in healthcare facilities can exacerbate sanitation and hygiene challenges. When facilities are overwhelmed with patients, it becomes more difficult to maintain cleanliness, adhere to hygiene protocols, and prevent the spread of infections. Inadequate spacing and limited resources can contribute to this issue.

4. Lack of Accountability

In some healthcare systems, there may be a lack of accountability for sanitation and hygiene standards. Without effective oversight and mechanisms to enforce compliance, healthcare facilities may struggle to prioritize these critical aspects of patient care.

Consequences of Poor Sanitation and Hygiene

1. Healthcare-Associated Infections (HAIs)

As mentioned earlier, poor sanitation and hygiene are significant contributors to HAIs. These infections can lead to additional illness, prolonged hospital stays, increased healthcare costs, and, tragically, patient deaths. HAIs are not only detrimental to individual patients but also strain healthcare systems.

2. Reduced Trust in Healthcare

Patients and their families may lose trust in healthcare facilities when they perceive inadequate sanitation and hygiene practices. This loss of trust can have long-lasting repercussions, as it may deter individuals from seeking necessary medical care, leading to delayed diagnoses and treatments.

3. Economic Burden

The economic burden of poor sanitation and hygiene in healthcare facilities is substantial. HAIs alone result in billions of dollars in additional healthcare costs globally each year. These costs include extended hospitalizations, additional treatments, and the use of expensive antibiotics.

Solutions to Improve Sanitation and Hygiene in Healthcare Facilities

1. Adequate Resource Allocation

To address the issue of poor sanitation and hygiene, healthcare systems must allocate sufficient resources to support these critical functions. This includes investing in infrastructure, staffing, and supplies necessary for maintaining cleanliness and infection control.

2. Comprehensive Training Programs

Healthcare workers should undergo comprehensive training programs focused on sanitation and hygiene practices. Training should encompass hand hygiene, proper use of PPE, aseptic techniques, and the importance of infection prevention. Continuous education and reinforcement are essential.

3. Implementation of Best Practices

Healthcare facilities should implement evidence-based best practices for sanitation and hygiene. This includes adopting standardized protocols for cleaning and disinfection, as well as routine monitoring and auditing to ensure compliance.

4. Promoting a Culture of Accountability

Creating a culture of accountability is crucial for sustaining improvements in sanitation and hygiene. This involves leadership commitment, clear policies, and mechanisms for reporting and addressing lapses in infection control.

5. Public Awareness Campaigns

Public awareness campaigns can help educate patients and their families about the importance of sanitation and hygiene in healthcare settings. Empowered and informed patients can advocate for their own safety and hold healthcare facilities accountable.

Success Stories and Case Studies

1. Case Study: The Clean Hands Initiative

In a hospital in a low-resource setting, the Clean Hands Initiative was launched to improve hand hygiene compliance among healthcare workers. The program included extensive training, the placement of hand hygiene stations at strategic locations, and regular performance audits. Over time, the hospital saw a significant reduction in HAIs and improved patient outcomes.

2. Success Story: Singapore General Hospital

Singapore General Hospital (SGH) is renowned for its stringent infection control measures. SGH attributes its success to a strong culture of infection control, where healthcare workers are educated, engaged, and empowered to enforce high standards of hygiene. SGH's approach includes continuous training, robust surveillance, and prompt intervention in case of breaches.

Conclusion

Poor sanitation and hygiene in healthcare facilities represent a critical challenge that impacts patient safety, healthcare outcomes, and healthcare systems at large. Recognizing the importance of sanitation and hygiene in healthcare settings is the first step toward addressing this issue effectively.

To improve sanitation and hygiene, healthcare systems must prioritize resource allocation, invest in comprehensive training, implement best practices, foster a culture of accountability, and engage in public awareness efforts. These measures, when executed with commitment and diligence, can lead to safer healthcare environments, reduced healthcare-associated infections, and ultimately better patient care.

In the journey to overcome the challenges of poor sanitation and hygiene in healthcare facilities, it is crucial that stakeholders at all levels – from policymakers and healthcare administrators to frontline workers and patients – come together to ensure that healthcare facilities truly fulfill their mission as places of healing and safety.

Introduction

Patient waiting times in government hospitals have been a long-standing issue that continues to plague healthcare systems worldwide. As we delve into the complexities of healthcare delivery, it becomes evident that extensive waiting times for treatment pose significant challenges for patients and healthcare providers alike. In this article, we will analyze the various challenges faced by patients who have to endure prolonged waiting times in government hospitals. We will also explore potential solutions to address these challenges and improve the overall quality of healthcare services.

Understanding the Significance of Patient Waiting Times

1. The Impact on Patient Health

Prolonged waiting times can have detrimental effects on patient health. Patients seeking immediate medical attention for critical conditions may experience deteriorating health while waiting for treatment. Delayed care can lead to worsening of illnesses, increased pain, and even fatalities in severe cases.

2. Psychological Distress

Waiting for extended periods in a healthcare facility can cause significant psychological distress. Patients often experience anxiety, frustration, and fear as they await their turn. This emotional toll can negatively affect their overall well-being.

3. Financial Burden

Prolonged waiting times can lead to increased out-of-pocket expenses for patients. They may need to take additional time off work, arrange for transportation, or spend on food and lodging while waiting. This financial burden disproportionately affects economically disadvantaged individuals.

Challenges Faced by Patients

1. Overcrowding

Overcrowding in government hospitals is a widespread issue, resulting in excessive waiting times. Limited resources, including beds and medical staff, contribute to this problem. Patients often have to wait for hours, if not days, to receive treatment due to the sheer volume of cases.

2. Inefficient Triage Systems

Triage systems are protocols and processes used in healthcare to prioritize the treatment of patients based on the severity of their medical condition, ensuring that resources are allocated efficiently during emergencies or high-demand situations. Triage systems are designed to prioritize patients based on the severity of their condition. However, inefficiencies in these systems can lead to incorrect prioritization, causing patients with critical illnesses to wait longer than they should.

3. Lack of Information

Patients waiting for treatment are often left in the dark about their estimated wait times. This lack of information can be frustrating and exacerbate anxiety. Clear communication regarding wait times and the patient's position in the queue can greatly alleviate this issue.

4. Inadequate Infrastructure

Many government hospitals suffer from outdated infrastructure and equipment. This leads to delays in diagnosis and treatment, as healthcare providers struggle to work with limited resources.

5. Staff Shortages

A shortage of healthcare professionals, including doctors and nurses, is a critical factor contributing to lengthy waiting times. Overworked staff members may struggle to meet the demands of a high patient load, resulting in delays in care.

6. Administrative Red Tape

Bureaucratic hurdles and administrative delays can further exacerbate patient waiting times. Obtaining necessary approvals, referrals, or insurance verifications can take an extended period, leaving patients in limbo.

Solutions to Improve Patient Waiting Times

1. Increase Funding for Healthcare

Adequate funding is essential for improving infrastructure, hiring more staff, and reducing overcrowding in government hospitals. Governments should prioritize healthcare budgets to ensure that hospitals have the necessary resources to provide timely care.

2. Enhance Triage Systems

Triage is a system used in healthcare settings, such as hospitals and emergency departments, to prioritize the allocation of medical care and resources based on the severity of patients' conditions. The primary goal of triage is to ensure that the most critically ill or injured patients receive prompt medical attention while efficiently managing the available healthcare resources. Streamlining and improving triage systems can help ensure that patients with critical conditions receive prompt attention. Regular training for healthcare staff on effective triage protocols is crucial.

3. Technology Integration

The integration of technology, such as electronic health records and appointment scheduling systems, can improve the efficiency of healthcare delivery. These systems can help reduce administrative delays and improve patient flow.

4. Staff Training and Development

Investing in the training and development of healthcare professionals is essential. This includes recruiting and training more doctors and nurses, as well as providing ongoing education to enhance their skills.

5. Public Awareness Campaigns

Public awareness campaigns can educate patients about their rights and responsibilities when seeking healthcare services. Empowered patients can make informed decisions and advocate for themselves, which can contribute to reducing waiting times.

6. Community Healthcare Centers

Establishing community healthcare centers can help alleviate the burden on government hospitals. These centers can provide primary care services, reducing the number of patients seeking treatment in overcrowded hospitals.

7. Telemedicine Services

Expanding telemedicine services can offer a solution for patients with non-urgent medical issues. This can reduce the physical load on hospitals and provide quicker access to healthcare advice.

8. Performance Monitoring and Accountability

Implementing systems to monitor hospital performance and hold healthcare providers accountable for long waiting times is crucial. Transparency in reporting waiting time data can motivate hospitals to improve their efficiency.

Conclusion

The challenges associated with patient waiting times in government hospitals are multifaceted and have significant implications for patient health, well-being, and financial stability. Addressing these challenges requires a holistic approach that involves adequate funding, improved infrastructure, staff training, and the integration of technology. Furthermore, empowering patients through education and awareness campaigns can help them navigate the healthcare system more effectively.

While there is no one-size-fits-all solution to the problem of patient waiting times, a concerted effort by governments, healthcare providers, and the community is essential to reduce these wait times and ensure that patients receive timely and efficient care. As we continue to analyze and address these challenges, it is our collective responsibility to prioritize the well-being of patients and strive for a healthcare system that is both accessible and efficient.

Introduction

The field of medicine has always been regarded as a noble profession, where individuals dedicate their lives to saving and improving the health of others. However, the medical field is not immune to challenges, and one significant issue that has been increasingly prominent in recent years is the safety of medical professionals. The rising incidents of violence against healthcare workers have brought this critical issue to the forefront. In this article, we will explore the safety concerns and incidents of violence against medical professionals, shedding light on the challenges they face and potential solutions.

The Alarming Rise in Violence

The safety of medical professionals has become a growing concern worldwide. In recent years, there has been a significant increase in incidents of violence against healthcare workers. This violence can take various forms, including physical assault, verbal abuse, threats, and even acts of vandalism against medical facilities. These incidents occur in a wide range of healthcare settings, from hospitals and clinics to ambulances and home healthcare.

1. Understanding the Causes

Several factors contribute to the rising violence against medical professionals. One of the primary causes is the heightened stress and frustration experienced by patients and their families. Long waiting times, concerns about treatment outcomes, financial burdens, and even misunderstandings can lead to heightened emotions, which sometimes result in violent outbursts.

Additionally, the healthcare system itself faces challenges, such as overcrowded emergency rooms, understaffed facilities, and resource limitations. These factors can exacerbate tensions and increase the risk of violence in healthcare settings.

2. The Impact of the Pandemic

The COVID-19 pandemic added a new layer of complexity to the issue of safety for medical professionals. Healthcare workers found themselves on the front lines of a global crisis, facing not only the usual challenges but also dealing with heightened anxiety and fear among patients and their families. The pandemic further strained healthcare resources and led to a surge in patient volumes, increasing the likelihood of confrontations and violence in hospitals.

The Consequences of Violence

Violence against medical professionals has far-reaching consequences that extend beyond the immediate physical and emotional harm inflicted on healthcare workers. These consequences affect the entire healthcare system and the quality of care provided to patients.

1. Physical and Psychological Impact

Medical professionals who experience violence often suffer physical injuries, ranging from minor bruises to severe trauma. The psychological impact can be equally devastating, leading to symptoms of anxiety, depression, post-traumatic stress disorder (PTSD), and burnout. This not only affects the well-being of healthcare workers but also impairs their ability to provide effective care.

2. Decreased Quality of Care

Violence in healthcare settings can disrupt the delivery of care. When medical professionals are fearful or anxious about their safety, their ability to focus on patient needs diminishes. This can result in errors, compromised patient outcomes, and a decrease in the overall quality of care.

3. Retention and Recruitment Challenges

The prevalence of violence in the medical field has also led to challenges in retaining and recruiting healthcare professionals. Many individuals are deterred from pursuing careers in healthcare due to concerns about their safety. Additionally, experienced medical professionals may choose to leave their positions or retire early to avoid the risk of violence, further exacerbating workforce shortages.

Addressing Safety Concerns

To address safety concerns and combat the alarming rise in violence against medical professionals, various strategies and solutions must be implemented.

1. Training and Education

One crucial step is to provide comprehensive training and education for healthcare workers on how to de-escalate tense situations, recognize early warning signs of potential violence, and respond effectively. This training can empower medical professionals to better handle challenging situations and protect themselves.

2. Improved Security Measures

Hospitals and healthcare facilities should invest in enhanced security measures to safeguard medical professionals. This may include the presence of security personnel, surveillance cameras, panic buttons, and secure access control systems. These measures can act as deterrents and provide immediate assistance in case of emergencies.

3. Enhanced Communication

Effective communication between medical professionals, patients, and their families is essential in preventing misunderstandings and reducing the risk of violence. Healthcare providers should prioritize clear and empathetic communication, ensuring that patients and their families are informed about treatment plans and expectations.

4. Support and Counseling Services

Recognizing the psychological toll of violence, healthcare organizations should provide access to support and counseling services for healthcare workers who have experienced violence or are at risk of burnout. These services can help individuals cope with trauma and stress, fostering resilience and well-being.

5. Legal Protections

Legislation should be in place to protect medical professionals from violence and ensure that perpetrators are held accountable for their actions. Legal measures can act as a deterrent and provide a means for healthcare workers to seek justice in cases of violence.

International Perspectives on Safety

Violence against medical professionals is not limited to a single country or region; it is a global issue that requires international attention and collaboration.

1. Experiences from Different Countries

Different countries have implemented various strategies to address violence against medical professionals. For example, in the United Kingdom, the National Health Service (NHS) has established a "zero tolerance" policy for violence against healthcare staff, with strict penalties for offenders. In Australia, there are public awareness campaigns to educate the community about the importance of respecting healthcare workers.

2. Collaborative Efforts

International organizations, such as the World Health Organization (WHO), can play a crucial role in raising awareness about the issue and facilitating collaboration between countries. Sharing best practices and strategies for preventing violence can help healthcare systems worldwide better protect their medical professionals.

The Way Forward

Addressing safety concerns and incidents of violence against medical professionals is an ongoing and multifaceted challenge. It requires the collective efforts of healthcare organizations, governments, policymakers, and the community.

1. Changing the Culture

A fundamental aspect of combating violence in healthcare settings is changing the culture surrounding interactions between patients, their families, and medical professionals. Promoting a culture of respect and empathy can go a long way in reducing the risk of violence.

2. Research and Data Collection

Continued research and data collection are essential to understand the scope and nature of violence against medical professionals fully. This information can inform the development of evidence-based interventions and policies.

3. Advocacy and Awareness

Advocacy efforts should focus on raising awareness about the issue of violence against medical professionals and mobilizing support from the community and policymakers. This can lead to greater recognition of the problem and the allocation of resources to address it.

4. Collaboration

Collaboration between healthcare organizations, law enforcement agencies, and government bodies is crucial in developing comprehensive strategies to protect medical professionals. Together, they can work to create safe environments in which healthcare workers can provide the best possible care to their patients.

Conclusion

The safety of medical professionals is a critical concern that must be addressed urgently. The rising incidents of violence against healthcare workers have significant consequences not only for the well-being of medical professionals but also for the quality of care provided to patients. By implementing training, security measures, and support services, as well as fostering a culture of respect and empathy, we can begin to reduce the incidence of violence in healthcare settings. International collaboration and advocacy efforts are essential in ensuring that medical professionals can continue to fulfill their noble mission of saving lives and improving health without fear for their safety. Only by addressing these challenges collectively can we create a safer and more supportive environment for those who dedicate their lives to the care of others in the medical field.

Introduction

The field of medicine is a complex and highly regulated industry, where healthcare professionals and institutions are expected to provide safe and effective care to patients. However, with this great responsibility comes a complex legal and regulatory landscape that governs various aspects of the medical field. In this article, we will explore two critical aspects of this landscape: malpractice and liability, and regulatory compliance. These areas are essential for healthcare providers and organizations to understand and navigate to ensure the highest quality of care while minimizing legal risks.

Understanding Medical Malpractice

Medical malpractice is a significant concern in the healthcare industry. It refers to the professional negligence or misconduct by healthcare providers that results in harm or injury to patients. Malpractice claims can have severe consequences for healthcare professionals and organizations, both in terms of reputation and financial liability.

1. Elements of Medical Malpractice

To establish a medical malpractice claim, four essential elements must be present.

Duty: The healthcare provider had a duty to provide care to the patient.

Breach of Duty: The provider breached their duty by failing to meet the standard of care.

Causation: The breach of duty directly caused harm or injury to the patient.

Damages: The patient suffered actual damages, such as physical or emotional harm.

2. Common Types of Medical Malpractice

Several common types of medical malpractice include misdiagnosis or delayed diagnosis, surgical errors, medication errors, and failure to obtain informed consent. Each of these can have devastating consequences for patients and lead to legal actions against healthcare professionals.

Liability in Healthcare

Liability in healthcare extends beyond medical malpractice and encompasses a broader range of legal responsibilities and obligations that healthcare providers and institutions must adhere to.

1. Types of Liability

Vicarious Liability: Healthcare organizations can be held liable for the actions of their employees or agents during the course of their employment.

Corporate Liability: Healthcare institutions can also face liability for issues related to corporate governance, compliance, and the quality of care provided.

Product Liability: Manufacturers of medical devices and pharmaceuticals can be held liable for defects or inadequate warnings related to their products.

2. Risk Management

Effective risk management strategies are crucial for mitigating liability in healthcare. This includes implementing protocols, training staff, and conducting regular audits to identify and address potential risks.

The Importance of Regulatory Compliance

Regulatory compliance is a cornerstone of healthcare governance. It involves adhering to federal, state, and local laws, as well as industry-specific regulations and standards. Compliance is essential for maintaining patient safety, ensuring quality of care, and avoiding legal consequences.

1. Federal Regulations

The Affordable Care Act (ACA): Enacted in 2010, the ACA introduced significant changes to healthcare regulation, including expanding access to care and implementing various quality and reporting requirements.

Health Insurance Portability and Accountability Act (HIPAA): HIPAA governs the privacy and security of patient health information, requiring strict safeguards to protect patient data.

ACA and HIPAA are both United States federal laws. Therefore, they are applicable exclusively in the United States. These laws do not apply to other countries, as they are specific to the U.S. healthcare system and healthcare-related regulations.

2. State Regulations

States often have their own healthcare regulations, including licensing requirements, scope of practice laws, and reporting obligations. Healthcare providers must comply with both federal and state regulations.

Regulatory Bodies

Various regulatory bodies oversee different aspects of healthcare compliance. These organizations play a critical role in setting and enforcing standards of care.

The Food and Drug Administration (FDA): The FDA regulates the safety and effectiveness of medical devices and pharmaceuticals, ensuring that they meet established standards before they can be marketed to the public.

The Centers for Medicare & Medicaid Services (CMS): CMS oversees federal healthcare programs, including Medicare and Medicaid, and sets reimbursement rates and quality standards for participating providers.

The Joint Commission: This independent, nonprofit organization accredits and certifies healthcare organizations and programs in the United States. Accreditation by the Joint Commission is often required for reimbursement and is a marker of quality in healthcare.

Both the FDA and CMS play critical roles in the U.S. healthcare system, with the FDA focused on product regulation and safety, and CMS primarily responsible for overseeing public healthcare programs and reimbursement. Their jurisdiction and authority are limited to the United States and its territories, and they do not have regulatory authority outside of the U.S. healthcare system.

Challenges in Regulatory Compliance

While regulatory compliance is crucial, it can be challenging for healthcare organizations to navigate the complex web of regulations effectively.

1. Evolving Regulations

Healthcare regulations are continually evolving, with new laws, guidelines, and standards being introduced regularly. Staying up-to-date and adapting to these changes is a constant challenge.

2. Resource Constraints

Complying with regulations often requires significant resources, including staff training, technology upgrades, and ongoing monitoring. Smaller healthcare providers may struggle to meet these requirements.

3. Data Security and Privacy

The increasing use of electronic health records (EHRs) and the digitalization of healthcare data have raised concerns about data security and privacy. Healthcare organizations must invest in robust cybersecurity measures to protect patient information.

Strategies for Navigating the Complex Landscape

Navigating the complex legal and regulatory landscape in healthcare requires a strategic approach that combines proactive risk management and a commitment to compliance.

1. Proactive Risk Management

Education and Training: Healthcare professionals should receive ongoing education and training to stay current with best practices and evolving regulations. This helps reduce the risk of malpractice and improve patient care.

Quality Assurance Programs: Implementing quality assurance programs, such as peer review processes and incident reporting systems, can help identify and address issues before they escalate into legal problems.

Informed Consent: Ensuring that patients fully understand the risks and benefits of medical procedures and treatments can help prevent claims of lack of informed consent.

2. Comprehensive Compliance Programs

Compliance Officers: Appointing a compliance officer or team responsible for monitoring and ensuring compliance with all relevant regulations can help healthcare organizations stay on track.

Regular Audits and Assessments: Conducting regular internal audits and assessments can help identify compliance gaps and address them promptly.

Technology Solutions: Investing in technology solutions that streamline compliance efforts, such as EHR systems with built-in security features, can enhance regulatory compliance. EHR (Electronic Health Record) systems are digital platforms that store and manage patients' health-related information, including medical histories, diagnoses, treatments, and other relevant data, to facilitate efficient and secure healthcare management and communication among healthcare providers.

3. Legal Support

Legal Counsel: Healthcare organizations should have legal counsel with expertise in healthcare law to provide guidance on compliance, risk management, and responding to legal issues.

Insurance Coverage: Maintaining appropriate malpractice insurance coverage is essential to protect against potential legal claims.

Conclusion

The legal and regulatory frameworks in the medical field are undeniably complex, but they are also crucial for ensuring patient safety, maintaining quality care, and minimizing legal risks. Healthcare providers and organizations must understand the intricacies of medical malpractice, liability, and regulatory compliance to navigate this landscape successfully.

By proactively managing risks, implementing comprehensive compliance programs, and seeking legal support when needed, healthcare professionals and institutions can provide the highest standard of care to their patients while safeguarding their own interests. In an ever-evolving healthcare environment, staying informed and adaptable is key to successfully meeting the challenges and responsibilities of the medical field.

Introduction

The field of medicine is rife with ethical dilemmas that challenge healthcare professionals, researchers, and policymakers alike. Two particularly intricate and emotionally charged areas are end-of-life care and research ethics. In this article, we will delve into the complexities of these ethical dilemmas, exploring the moral terrain they present and the strategies for navigating them. Both issues require careful consideration of patient autonomy, beneficence (an ethical principle that emphasizes the obligation to act in the best interests of the patients and to promote their well-being), non-maleficence (an ethical principle that emphasizes the obligation to "do no harm" to the patients), and justice, making them crucial topics for discussion and reflection in the medical field.

End-of-Life Care

End-of-life care, also known as palliative care or hospice care, refers to a type of medical and emotional support provided to individuals who are nearing the end of their lives, typically due to a terminal illness or advanced age. The primary goal of end-of-life care is to ensure that the patient experiences comfort, dignity, and the highest possible quality of life during their final stages, while also providing support and guidance to their families.

End-of-life care presents a profound ethical challenge: how to balance patient autonomy with the principle of beneficence. Autonomy, the patient's right to make decisions about their own medical treatment, often comes into sharp focus as individuals face life-threatening illnesses. Simultaneously, healthcare professionals are tasked with providing the best possible care to promote the patient's well-being, a concept deeply ingrained in the principle of beneficence.

1. The Role of Advance Directives

Advance directives, including living wills (documents in which individuals outline their preferences for medical treatment, such as life-sustaining measures) and do-not-resuscitate (DNR) orders (directives specifying the withholding of cardiopulmonary resuscitation, or CPR), establish a legal framework for patients to communicate their end-of-life care preferences in situations where they are unable to make decisions. This respects autonomy by ensuring that healthcare decisions align with the patient's stated wishes. However, it can also pose challenges when the patient's wishes conflict with what healthcare professionals believe is in their best interest.

2. The Case of Medical Futility

Medical futility is a contentious issue within end-of-life care ethics. It arises when healthcare providers believe that a particular treatment is unlikely to benefit the patient, yet the patient or their family insists on its continuation. In such cases, the principle of beneficence collides with patient autonomy, raising questions about who should have the final say in treatment decisions.

3. Open and Honest Communication

Navigating these ethical dilemmas requires open and honest communication between healthcare providers, patients, and their families. Transparent discussions can help align the patient's preferences with what is medically feasible and ethically justifiable, finding a middle ground that respects both autonomy and beneficence.

Research Ethics

Research in the medical field is essential for advancing knowledge, developing new treatments, and improving patient outcomes. However, it must be conducted ethically and responsibly, with a primary focus on protecting the rights and well-being of research participants. Vulnerable populations, such as children, prisoners, and those with limited decision-making capacity, pose unique ethical challenges in the realm of research.

1. Informed Consent and Vulnerable Populations

Obtaining informed consent is a fundamental ethical principle in research. However, vulnerable populations may have diminished capacity to provide informed consent due to their age, cognitive impairments, or other factors. Balancing the need for research with the duty to protect these individuals presents a complex ethical dilemma.

2. Beneficence and Non-Maleficence in Research

The principles of beneficence and non-maleficence require that researchers maximize benefits and minimize harm to participants. In the case of vulnerable populations, the potential for exploitation and harm is heightened. Researchers must navigate the delicate balance of advancing medical knowledge while safeguarding the well-being of vulnerable participants.

3. Justice and Equitable Research

Justice in research demands that participants are treated fairly and that the benefits and burdens of research are distributed equitably. Vulnerable populations are often at risk of being disproportionately included in research projects due to convenience or accessibility. Ensuring equitable representation in research while respecting their vulnerabilities is a crucial ethical challenge.

Strategies for Navigating Ethical Dilemmas

Navigating the ethical dilemmas in end-of-life care and research ethics requires a thoughtful and principled approach. Several strategies can help healthcare professionals and researchers make morally sound decisions in these complex domains.

1. Ethical Committees and Consultations

In both end-of-life care and research, ethical committees play a vital role in providing guidance and oversight. These committees consist of experts in ethics, law, medicine, and other relevant fields who can review cases and offer ethical analysis and recommendations. Seeking their input can help resolve difficult dilemmas.

2. Ethical Frameworks and Guidelines

Ethical frameworks and guidelines, such as the principles outlined in the Belmont Report and the World Medical Association's Declaration of Helsinki, provide valuable guidance for making ethically sound decisions in research. Healthcare institutions often have their own ethical guidelines for end-of-life care, which can serve as a reference point for professionals.

3. Interdisciplinary Collaboration

Ethical dilemmas in medicine often benefit from interdisciplinary collaboration. Involving healthcare providers, ethicists, legal experts, and patient advocates in discussions and decision-making processes can offer a more comprehensive perspective and help strike a balance between conflicting principles.

4. Continuous Education and Training

Continuous education and training in ethics are essential for healthcare professionals and researchers. Keeping up-to-date with the latest ethical developments and case studies can enhance their ability to navigate complex dilemmas with wisdom and sensitivity.

Conclusion

Ethical dilemmas in medicine, particularly in end-of-life care and research ethics, require healthcare professionals and researchers to tread carefully through complex moral terrain. The delicate balance between patient autonomy, beneficence, non-maleficence, and justice demands thoughtful consideration and principled decision-making. By engaging ethical committees, adhering to established frameworks, collaborating across disciplines, and investing in ongoing education, we can better navigate these challenges and ensure that our medical practices and research efforts uphold the highest ethical standards. In doing so, we honor the principles that underpin our profession and advance the well-being of those we serve.

Chapter 14. Mental Health and Well-being of Healthcare Workers

Introduction

The field of healthcare is often portrayed as a noble and rewarding profession, where dedicated individuals selflessly care for the sick and vulnerable. While this perception is undoubtedly accurate, it often glosses over the significant challenges that healthcare workers face in their daily lives. This article explores the critical issue of mental health and well-being among healthcare workers, with a particular focus on burnout, stress, and the importance of support systems.

The Burden of Healthcare Work

1. The Noble Calling

Healthcare professionals, including doctors, nurses, and allied healthcare workers, are indeed dedicated to a noble calling. Their commitment to healing and saving lives is unparalleled, making them the backbone of any society's well-being. However, this dedication often comes at a cost.

2. The Toll on Mental Health

Healthcare work is emotionally and physically demanding, leading to high levels of stress and burnout among practitioners. Long hours, emotional strain, and exposure to illness and death take a toll on the mental health of these professionals, affecting their well-being and job satisfaction.

Burnout: The Silent Epidemic

1. Understanding Burnout

Burnout is a pervasive issue among healthcare workers. It is characterized by emotional exhaustion, depersonalization, and a diminished sense of personal accomplishment. Burnout can result from chronic stress, heavy workloads, and an inability to cope with the demands of the profession.

2. The Causes of Burnout

Several factors contribute to burnout among healthcare workers.

Heavy Workloads: Healthcare professionals often face long hours, frequent shifts, and high patient-to-staff ratios, leaving them physically and mentally exhausted.

Emotional Demands: Dealing with patients' pain, suffering, and sometimes death can be emotionally draining. Healthcare workers must manage their own emotions while providing compassionate care.

Administrative Burdens: Excessive paperwork, administrative tasks, and bureaucratic hurdles add to the workload, diverting time and energy away from patient care.

Lack of Autonomy: Some healthcare workers feel disempowered due to rigid protocols and lack of control over their work environment, leading to frustration and burnout.

3. The Consequences of Burnout

Burnout can have severe consequences for both healthcare workers and patients.

Reduced Quality of Care: Burnout may lead to errors, decreased attentiveness, and compromised patient safety.

Attrition: Many healthcare professionals leave the field prematurely due to burnout, exacerbating workforce shortages.

Mental Health Issues: Burnout is linked to mental health problems such as depression, anxiety, and substance abuse among healthcare workers.

Stress in the Healthcare Sector

1. The Constant Stressors

Healthcare workers face a myriad of stressors, including:

High-Stakes Decisions: Medical professionals must make critical decisions that can have life-or-death consequences, adding immense pressure.

Work-Life Imbalance: Long hours and unpredictable schedules can disrupt personal lives, leading to stress and strain on relationships.

Traumatic Events: Witnessing trauma and death on a regular basis can lead to post-traumatic stress disorder (PTSD) in healthcare workers.

Ethical Dilemmas: Professionals often grapple with ethical dilemmas, such as resource allocation during a crisis, which can be emotionally distressing.

2. Coping Mechanisms

While stress is inevitable in healthcare, healthcare workers can adopt strategies to mitigate its impact.

Self-Care: Prioritizing self-care through exercise, mindfulness, and hobbies can help manage stress.

Support Networks: Building strong support networks with colleagues and seeking professional help when needed can provide a vital outlet for stress.

Training and Education: Healthcare institutions can offer training in stress management and resilience-building to equip their staff with effective coping skills.

Support Systems for Healthcare Workers

1. Institutional Support

Healthcare organizations have a crucial role in supporting the mental health of their staff.

Mental Health Services: Offering accessible mental health services within healthcare settings can provide immediate support to those in need.

Workload Management: Implementing reasonable workloads and schedules can prevent burnout and excessive stress.

Training Programs: **Providing** training in communication, emotional intelligence, and stress management can empower healthcare workers to better cope with their demanding roles.

2. Peer Support

Peer support programs within healthcare institutions can be highly effective.

Peer Counseling: **Healthcare** workers can benefit from talking to peers who understand the unique challenges of the profession.

Support Groups: **Organizing** support groups for healthcare workers to share their experiences and coping strategies can foster a sense of community.

3. Mental Health Initiatives

Promoting mental health initiatives can create a culture of well-being within the healthcare sector.

Mental Health Awareness Campaigns: **Raising** awareness about mental health issues and reducing stigma can encourage healthcare workers to seek help when needed.

Resilience Training: **Teaching** healthcare workers resilience skills can help them bounce back from adversity and manage stress effectively.

The Role of Policy and Advocacy

1. Government and Policy

Government bodies and policymakers play a crucial role in addressing the mental health of healthcare workers.

Legislation: Enacting legislation that mandates mental health support and worker protection can provide a legal framework for addressing these issues.

Funding: Allocating resources for mental health programs within healthcare institutions can ensure sustainable support.

2. Professional Associations

Professional associations can advocate for their members' mental health and well-being.

Guidelines: Developing guidelines and best practices for mental health support within the profession can set standards for healthcare institutions.

Research and Education: Investing in research on healthcare worker mental health and providing educational resources can raise awareness and drive change.

The Way Forward

1. Changing the Culture

Transforming the culture within the healthcare sector is essential.

Open Conversations: Encouraging open conversations about mental health and stress can reduce stigma and normalize seeking help.

Holistic Approaches: Adopting a holistic approach to healthcare that includes mental well-being as a priority can benefit both workers and patients.

2. Collective Responsibility

Addressing the mental health and well-being of healthcare workers is a collective responsibility.

Collaboration: Healthcare institutions, governments, professional associations, and individuals must collaborate to create a supportive ecosystem.

Continuous Improvement: Recognizing that the mental health landscape is dynamic, efforts to support healthcare workers should be ongoing and adaptive.

Conclusion

The mental health and well-being of healthcare workers are of paramount importance, not only for their own sake but also for the quality of care they provide to patients. Burnout and stress are formidable challenges that demand proactive solutions. By implementing support systems at institutional, peer, and societal levels, and by advocating for policy changes, we can ensure that healthcare workers receive the support they need to thrive in their noble profession while safeguarding their mental health. The journey towards a healthier healthcare workforce is a shared responsibility that benefits us all.

Introduction

The COVID-19 pandemic has been a global wake-up call, revealing the vulnerabilities and shortcomings of our healthcare systems and public health infrastructure. It has underscored the critical importance of effective pandemic preparedness and vaccine distribution. This article delves into the lessons learned from the COVID-19 pandemic in these two crucial areas and discusses the challenges and solutions that have emerged during these trying times.

Pandemic Preparedness

1. Pandemic Preparedness

Before COVID-19, pandemic preparedness was often seen as a theoretical exercise, with many countries ill-equipped to handle a global health crisis of such magnitude. The pandemic exposed the inadequacies of our preparedness efforts, prompting a global reckoning.

Inadequate Stockpiles and Supply Chains

The COVID-19 pandemic highlighted the fragility of supply chains for essential medical supplies and personal protective equipment (PPE). Many nations faced shortages, revealing the necessity for robust stockpiles and diversified supply sources.

Solution: Strengthening Supply Chains

Countries are now focusing on diversifying their supply sources, building strategic stockpiles of critical medical equipment, and establishing international partnerships for smoother resource sharing during crises.

2. Data Sharing and Surveillance

Timely and accurate data sharing among countries is crucial for early detection and containment of pandemics. The lack of transparency in the initial stages of the COVID-19 outbreak hindered response efforts.

Solution: Enhanced Data Sharing

The pandemic has prompted calls for improved international cooperation in sharing data and information related to infectious disease outbreaks. Initiatives like the WHO's Global Outbreak Alert and Response Network (GOARN) aim to facilitate data sharing and coordination.

3. Vaccine Research and Development

The rapid development of COVID-19 vaccines was a remarkable achievement, but it also exposed the need for a more proactive approach to vaccine research and development for emerging pathogens.

Solution: Investment in Vaccine Research

Governments and organizations are investing in research platforms that can be quickly adapted for new pathogens. The Coalition for Epidemic Preparedness Innovations (CEPI) is a prime example, focusing on accelerating vaccine development.

Vaccine Distribution

COVID-19 Vaccine Distribution

The distribution of COVID-19 vaccines has raised significant ethical and logistical challenges, emphasizing the importance of equitable access to vaccines for all.

1. Vaccine Nationalism

Some countries adopted a vaccine nationalism approach, securing large quantities of vaccines for their citizens while leaving others with limited access. This approach has been widely criticized for exacerbating global health inequalities.

Solution: Vaccine Equity

COVAX, short for "COVID-19 Vaccines Global Access," is a global initiative aimed at ensuring equitable access to COVID-19 vaccines. Wealthier nations must support these initiatives and commit to fair distribution.

2. Supply Chain Challenges

The distribution of vaccines on a global scale requires complex supply chains and cold storage facilities, posing challenges for many countries, particularly in resource-limited settings.

Solution: Infrastructure Investment

Investing in supply chain infrastructure, particularly in low- and middle-income countries, is essential to ensure the efficient distribution of vaccines during future pandemics.

3. Vaccine Hesitancy

Vaccine hesitancy, fueled by misinformation and mistrust, has hindered vaccination efforts. Building public trust in vaccines is vital for achieving herd immunity.

Solution: Vaccine Education

Health authorities and governments must prioritize vaccine education campaigns, addressing concerns and providing accurate information to combat vaccine hesitancy effectively.

Lessons from Success Stories

While the COVID-19 pandemic brought numerous challenges, it also showcased several success stories in pandemic preparedness and vaccine distribution.

1. New Vaccine Technologies

The development of mRNA vaccines, such as those produced by Pfizer-BioNTech and Moderna, demonstrated the potential of cutting-edge vaccine technologies. These platforms can be adapted quickly to respond to emerging threats.

2. South Korea's Testing and Tracing

South Korea's rapid and widespread testing, contact tracing, and quarantine measures proved highly effective in controlling the spread of COVID-19 without resorting to strict lockdowns.

3. New Zealand's Elimination Strategy

New Zealand's elimination strategy, often referred to as "COVID-19 elimination" or "zero-COVID," is a public health approach aimed at completely eliminating the presence of the COVID-19 virus within the country's borders. This strategy involves a combination of strict border controls, rigorous testing and contact tracing, quarantine and isolation measures, public health campaigns, and, at times, regional or national lockdowns.

4. Global Collaborations

Collaborations on an international scale, which encompassed pharmaceutical companies, governments, and global initiatives like COVAX, exemplified the potency of worldwide cooperation in the development and equitable distribution of vaccines.

The Way Forward

Lessons from the COVID-19 pandemic offer valuable insights into improving pandemic preparedness and vaccine distribution for future health crises.

1. Global Solidarity

The pandemic has underscored the need for global solidarity in the face of health crises. International cooperation, data sharing, and equitable vaccine distribution should be prioritized.

2. Investment in Healthcare Infrastructure

Countries must invest in healthcare infrastructure, including supply chains, cold storage, and testing capacity, to better respond to future pandemics.

3. Research and Development

Increased funding and support for research and development of vaccines and treatments for emerging pathogens are essential to ensure a rapid response to future health threats.

4. Public Health Education

Efforts to combat vaccine hesitancy and misinformation should continue, emphasizing the importance of vaccination in protecting individuals and communities.

Conclusion

The COVID-19 pandemic has been a harsh teacher, revealing weaknesses in our pandemic preparedness and vaccine distribution systems. However, it has also provided an opportunity to learn from our mistakes and improve our approach to global health crises. By prioritizing international cooperation, equity in vaccine access, and investment in healthcare infrastructure, we can better prepare for and respond to future public health challenges. The lessons learned from the COVID-19 pandemic will undoubtedly shape the future of healthcare and our ability to safeguard the well-being of the global population.

Introduction

The healthcare industry is facing a critical challenge - balancing quality and affordability. As the costs of healthcare continue to escalate, it has become imperative to find sustainable solutions that ensure access to high-quality care while also making it affordable for all. In this article, we will delve into the escalating healthcare costs, the economics behind healthcare, and explore potential solutions to strike a balance between quality and affordability.

Understanding the Escalating Healthcare Costs

1. Rising Healthcare Expenditure

The first and foremost concern is the incessant increase in healthcare expenditure. In recent years, healthcare costs have been growing at an alarming rate, outpacing inflation and wage growth. This rise is attributed to various factors, including technological advancements, an aging population, and the prevalence of chronic diseases.

2. Administrative Overhead

Administrative overhead in healthcare is another significant contributor to escalating costs. The complex billing systems, bureaucracy, and the need for extensive record-keeping inflate expenses. Streamlining administrative processes can potentially reduce these costs.

3. Pharmaceutical Costs

The cost of pharmaceuticals is a contentious issue within healthcare economics. High drug prices, often driven by research and development expenses, have a direct impact on overall healthcare expenses. The balance between innovation and affordability must be struck here.

4. Medical Technology

While medical advancements have led to improved patient outcomes, they have also driven up costs. Cutting-edge medical equipment and procedures can be expensive, necessitating a careful evaluation of their cost-effectiveness.

Healthcare Economics

1. Supply and Demand Dynamics

The principles of supply and demand play a crucial role in healthcare economics. The scarcity of healthcare resources, including physicians and hospital beds, can lead to higher costs when demand exceeds supply. This imbalance often results in higher prices for medical services.

2. Third-Party Payers

Many healthcare systems involve third-party payers, such as insurance companies and government programs like Medicare and Medicaid. These payers negotiate prices with healthcare providers, impacting the overall economics of healthcare. The effectiveness of these negotiations can significantly affect the affordability of care.

3. Fee-for-Service vs. Value-Based Care

Fee-for-Service is a healthcare payment model in which providers receive payment for each medical service or procedure they perform, regardless of the patient's health outcome. Value-Based Care is a healthcare payment and delivery model that rewards healthcare providers based on the quality and effectiveness of care they provide, rather than solely on the quantity of services rendered.

Traditionally, the fee-for-service model incentivized healthcare providers to perform more procedures, potentially leading to overutilization and higher costs. Shifting towards value-based care, which focuses on outcomes rather than services provided, has gained traction as a way to control costs while maintaining quality.

4. Cost-Sharing

Deductibles are fixed amounts that insured individuals must pay out of pocket for covered healthcare services before their insurance plan starts covering costs, typically on an annual basis. Copayments (or copays) are predetermined, fixed amounts that insured individuals are required to pay for specific healthcare services or prescriptions at the time of service, with the insurance plan covering the remaining costs.

Cost-sharing mechanisms, such as deductibles and copayments, are intended to make patients more conscious of their healthcare spending. However, excessive cost-sharing can deter individuals from seeking necessary care, raising concerns about the accessibility of healthcare services.

Solutions for Balancing Quality and Affordability

1. Preventive Care and Health Education

One of the most effective strategies for controlling healthcare costs is investing in preventive care and health education. Encouraging a healthy lifestyle and early intervention can prevent costly chronic conditions and reduce the overall burden on the healthcare system.

2. Telemedicine and Digital Health

The adoption of telemedicine and digital health technologies has the potential to increase access to care while reducing costs. Virtual consultations, remote monitoring, and electronic health records streamline healthcare delivery and can eliminate unnecessary office visits.

3. Price Transparency

Promoting price transparency in healthcare is essential to empower consumers to make informed choices. When patients have access to information about the cost of medical services and procedures, they can compare prices and make cost-effective decisions.

4. Value-Based Payment Models

Transitioning to value-based payment models aligns the incentives of healthcare providers with patient outcomes. By rewarding quality and efficiency rather than the quantity of services, these models can improve care while controlling costs.

5. Government Interventions

Government intervention in the form of price controls and regulations on drug pricing can help address the issue of skyrocketing pharmaceutical costs. These measures can ensure that essential medications remain affordable for the general population.

6. Healthcare Innovation

Encouraging innovation in healthcare can lead to cost-effective solutions. This includes investing in research and development of new medical technologies and treatment methods that improve outcomes without inflating costs.

7. Streamlining Administrative Processes

Reducing administrative overhead through the adoption of electronic health records and standardized billing practices can simplify healthcare operations and reduce unnecessary costs.

8. Global Budgeting

Implementing global budgeting, where healthcare systems are allocated a fixed budget, can encourage efficiency and cost-consciousness. However, careful planning and resource allocation are essential to prevent underfunding of critical services.

Conclusion

The challenge of balancing quality and affordability in healthcare is a complex and multifaceted issue. Escalating healthcare costs, driven by various factors, threaten the accessibility of care for many individuals and communities.

Understanding the economics of healthcare, including supply and demand dynamics, third-party payer systems, and different payment models, is crucial in addressing these challenges.

Solutions must encompass preventive care, digital health technologies, price transparency, value-based payment models, and government interventions to regulate drug pricing. Additionally, streamlining administrative processes and encouraging innovation are key components of achieving a sustainable healthcare system.

Ultimately, finding the right balance between quality and affordability in healthcare requires a collaborative effort from policymakers, healthcare providers, insurance companies, and patients. By implementing these solutions and working together, we can ensure that healthcare remains accessible and of high quality for everyone, regardless of their economic status.

Introduction

The healthcare sector plays a pivotal role in society, aiming to provide medical services, promote public health, and ensure the overall well-being of the population. Healthcare systems around the world can be broadly categorized into two main types: private and government-funded (often referred to as public). Each of these systems has its own set of characteristics, strengths, and challenges. In this article, we will delve into the private and government healthcare systems, analyze their key differences, and explore the challenges they face. Understanding these differences and challenges is essential for developing effective solutions to improve healthcare delivery for all.

Private Healthcare

Private healthcare refers to a system where healthcare services are primarily provided by privately-owned institutions, and individuals often pay for these services either through insurance or out-of-pocket expenses. Here are the key characteristics of private healthcare.

1. Ownership and Management

Private healthcare facilities are typically owned and operated by for-profit organizations or individuals. This means that the primary focus is on generating revenue while providing quality healthcare services.

2. Access and Cost

Access to private healthcare often depends on an individual's ability to pay for services. Private healthcare is known for its high cost, which can create barriers to access for lower-income individuals or those without adequate insurance coverage.

3. Quality and Innovation

Private healthcare providers compete for patients, which can drive innovation and the pursuit of high-quality care. They often invest in advanced medical technologies and facilities to attract patients seeking premium services.

4. Patient Choice

Patients in private healthcare systems generally have more choice and control over their healthcare providers and treatment options. They can choose their doctors, hospitals, and treatment plans based on their preferences and financial capabilities.

Government Healthcare

Government healthcare, on the other hand, is a system in which the government is the primary provider or regulator of healthcare services. This system is often funded through taxation and aims to provide healthcare services to all citizens. Here are the key characteristics of government healthcare.

1. Universal Access

Government healthcare systems strive to provide equal access to healthcare services for all citizens, regardless of their income or social status. The goal is to ensure that healthcare is a basic right and not a privilege.

2. Publicly Funded

Government healthcare is typically funded through taxation, and the government plays a central role in financing, organizing, and overseeing healthcare services. This funding model aims to reduce or eliminate financial barriers to healthcare.

3. Cost Control

Government healthcare systems often have mechanisms in place to control healthcare costs. This can include price controls, negotiations with pharmaceutical companies, and cost-effective treatment guidelines.

4. Quality Assurance

While government healthcare systems prioritize accessibility, they also strive to maintain high-quality standards of care. Regulatory bodies and guidelines are established to ensure that healthcare providers meet certain quality benchmarks.

Challenges Faced by Private Healthcare

Private healthcare systems offer many advantages, such as innovation and choice, but they also face several significant challenges.

1. Cost Barriers

The high cost of private healthcare can be a significant barrier for many individuals. Those without adequate insurance coverage or financial resources may delay or forgo necessary medical treatment, leading to negative health outcomes.

2. Inequality in Access

Private healthcare systems often perpetuate inequality in access to healthcare. Those who can afford premium insurance plans or out-of-pocket expenses may receive faster and more comprehensive care than those with limited resources.

3. Profit Motive

The profit motive in private healthcare can sometimes lead to overuse of medical services, unnecessary treatments, and high healthcare costs. This can result in healthcare becoming a business rather than a service aimed at improving health.

4. Insurance Complexities

Dealing with private health insurance can be complex and confusing for patients. Understanding coverage, copayments, deductibles, and out-of-network costs can be challenging, leading to misunderstandings and unexpected expenses.

Challenges Faced by Government Healthcare

Government healthcare systems strive for universal access and cost control, but they also face their own set of challenges.

1. Budget Constraints

Government healthcare systems are often constrained by limited budgets, which can lead to long wait times for certain treatments or limited access to advanced technologies and treatments.

2. Bureaucracy and Red Tape

Government-run healthcare can be bureaucratic, with administrative inefficiencies that can slow down decision-making and hinder the delivery of care.

3. Provider Shortages

In some government healthcare systems, there may be shortages of healthcare providers due to budget limitations. This can result in overworked medical professionals and reduced quality of care.

4. Limited Choice

While government healthcare systems aim to provide access to essential services, patients may have limited choice in selecting healthcare providers and treatment options compared to the private sector.

Solutions and Innovations

To address the challenges faced by both private and government healthcare systems, various solutions and innovations have been proposed and implemented.

1. Universal Healthcare Coverage

Many countries are exploring ways to achieve universal healthcare coverage, which combines the strengths of both private and government systems. This approach aims to provide basic healthcare services to all citizens while allowing the option for individuals to purchase additional private insurance for enhanced services.

2. Telemedicine and Digital Health

Both private and government healthcare systems are increasingly embracing telemedicine and digital health solutions to improve access to care, especially in remote or underserved areas. These technologies can reduce costs and enhance the patient experience.

3. Preventive Healthcare Programs

Governments and private healthcare providers are investing in preventive healthcare programs to reduce the burden of chronic diseases and improve overall public health. These programs can lead to long-term cost savings and better outcomes.

4. Public-Private Partnerships

Collaborations between private and government healthcare sectors can lead to innovative solutions. For example, private hospitals may provide specialized services to alleviate the burden on government-funded facilities.

5. Health Information Exchange

Implementing health information exchange systems can improve the coordination of care between different healthcare providers and reduce redundancy in testing and treatment, ultimately improving the quality of care.

Conclusion

Private and government healthcare systems have their own strengths and challenges. While private healthcare can offer choice and innovation, it often comes at a high cost, potentially excluding those with limited financial means. Government healthcare systems prioritize accessibility and cost control but can sometimes face budget constraints and bureaucratic inefficiencies.

The future of healthcare may lie in finding a balance between these two models, where universal access to basic healthcare services is ensured, and individuals have the option to supplement their coverage with private insurance for additional benefits. Additionally, embracing digital health technologies, preventive healthcare programs, and public-private partnerships can lead to more efficient and effective healthcare systems.

Ultimately, the goal of any healthcare system should be to provide high-quality care that is accessible and affordable for all citizens, regardless of their socioeconomic status. By analyzing the differences and challenges faced by private and government healthcare, we can work towards creating a more equitable and efficient healthcare system that meets the needs of the population.

Chapter 18. Unnecessary Surgeries and Excessive Medical Testing

Introduction

The field of medicine is often regarded as a noble profession, one that is primarily driven by a commitment to healing and alleviating suffering. However, beneath the veneer of this noble endeavor, there exists a darker side - cases of unnecessary surgeries and excessive medical testing, motivated by financial gain rather than genuine patient need. In this article, we delve into these ethical challenges in the medical field, shedding light on some disconcerting instances and exploring potential solutions.

Unnecessary Surgeries

1. Defining the Problem

Uncovering the prevalence of unnecessary surgeries is a disturbing revelation in modern healthcare. These surgeries, driven by financial motives, compromise the trust patients place in their healthcare providers. The motivations behind such surgeries are often profit-centric, prioritizing the financial gain of healthcare institutions and professionals over the best interests of patients.

2. Case Studies

The scandal of unnecessary cardiac stent insertions is a glaring example of this issue. Cardiologists, motivated by financial incentives, performed invasive procedures that were medically unwarranted, exposing patients to unnecessary risks.

Similarly, the alarming practice of unwarranted hysterectomies (a surgical procedure to remove the uterus, often performed for medical reasons such as uterine fibroids or gynecological cancers) has shattered trust in healthcare. Patients, often unaware of alternatives, have undergone life-altering surgeries without clear medical necessity.

Orthopedic procedures, such as joint replacements and spinal surgeries, are also susceptible to overutilization. In some instances, patients have been subjected to surgeries that could have been avoided with a second opinion or non-surgical interventions.

Factors Encouraging Unnecessary Surgeries

❖ Financial incentives in fee-for-service healthcare models are a significant driver of unnecessary surgeries. When healthcare providers are compensated based on the volume of services they deliver, the temptation to recommend procedures, even when not entirely justified, becomes more significant.

❖ Defensive medicine, motivated by the fear of malpractice lawsuits, also contributes to this problem. Healthcare professionals may lean towards overtreating patients to avoid potential legal repercussions.

❖ The lack of clear clinical guidelines for certain procedures leaves room for interpretation and overuse.

Solutions

❖ To combat the issue of unnecessary surgeries, shifting to value-based care models is crucial. In value-based care, providers are rewarded for delivering high-quality care that improves patient outcomes, rather than being reimbursed for the number of procedures performed.

- ❖ Enhanced oversight and regulation can help identify and penalize healthcare professionals and institutions engaged in unnecessary surgeries.

- ❖ Promoting the practice of seeking second opinions for elective surgeries can empower patients to make more informed decisions about their healthcare.

Excessive Medical Testing

1. Understanding the Issue

The rise of overtesting in modern healthcare has raised concerns about patient well-being. Excessive medical testing, driven by various factors, can lead to unnecessary patient anxiety, increased healthcare costs, and exposure to potential harm.

2. Case Studies

- ❖ The CT scan conundrum highlights the risks of excessive testing. Frequent CT scans expose patients to ionizing radiation, increasing the risk of cancer. However, the diagnostic benefits may not always outweigh these risks.

- ❖ Overutilization of advanced imaging technologies, such as MRI and PET scans, has become a common practice. These expensive tests are often ordered without clear medical indications, contributing to rising healthcare costs.

❖ Overdiagnosis and overtreatment in cancer screening, such as mammography and prostate-specific antigen (PSA) testing, can lead to unnecessary treatments and psychological distress for patients.

Drivers of Excessive Testing

❖ Defensive medicine, driven by the fear of missed diagnoses and potential lawsuits, plays a significant role in excessive medical testing. Healthcare providers may order numerous tests to avoid any allegations of negligence.

❖ Financial incentives for healthcare providers can encourage overtesting, as more tests can mean higher reimbursement.

❖ Patient demand for more tests, often influenced by the belief that more testing equates to better care, contributes to this issue.

Solutions

❖ Promoting shared decision-making between doctors and patients is essential. Engaging patients in discussions about the risks and benefits of diagnostic tests can help reduce unnecessary testing.

❖ Developing evidence-based guidelines for diagnostic testing can provide clarity to healthcare providers and reduce variability in testing practices.

❖ Implementing stricter utilization review processes within healthcare institutions can help identify and discourage the overuse of diagnostic tests.

Conclusion

Unnecessary surgeries and excessive medical testing pose significant ethical challenges in the medical field, undermining the fundamental principle of patient-centered care. To address these issues, healthcare systems, providers, and policymakers must collaborate to shift the focus from profit to patient well-being. By implementing evidence-based guidelines, fostering a culture of shared decision-making, and reforming healthcare reimbursement models, we can work toward a healthcare system that prioritizes the best interests of patients above all else. In doing so, we can hope to restore trust in medicine and ensure that every medical intervention is motivated by a genuine commitment to healing and improving lives.

Chapter 19. Solutions and Recommendations

Introduction

The preceding chapters have painted a comprehensive picture of the myriad challenges that the medical field faces today. From workforce shortages and disparities in access to healthcare to issues of inadequate infrastructure and rising costs, these challenges are complex and intertwined. Finding practical solutions is paramount to ensuring the continued growth and effectiveness of the healthcare sector. In this chapter, we will delve into a range of solutions and recommendations to tackle the issues highlighted in earlier chapters.

1. Strengthening Education and Training

Solution: Promote Interdisciplinary Education

One way to address workforce shortages and enhance the quality of healthcare is to encourage interdisciplinary education. This approach fosters collaboration among healthcare professionals and equips them with a broader skill set. By breaking down traditional silos, it enables more efficient care delivery.

Recommendation: Expand Online and Remote Learning

To meet the growing demand for healthcare workers, institutions should embrace online and remote learning methods. This not only provides access to education for a wider audience but also allows healthcare professionals to update their skills without leaving their workplaces.

2. Improving Access to Healthcare

Solution: Telemedicine and Telehealth Services

Leveraging technology, telemedicine and telehealth services can bridge the gap in healthcare access, especially in remote or underserved areas. Governments and healthcare providers should invest in telemedicine infrastructure and ensure it reaches those in need.

Recommendation: Mobile Clinics and Outreach Programs

To reach marginalized communities, mobile clinics and outreach programs can provide essential healthcare services. These initiatives can bring medical professionals and resources directly to areas with limited access to healthcare facilities.

3. Upgrading Medical Infrastructure

Solution: Infrastructure Investment

Governments and private entities should invest in upgrading medical infrastructure, including hospitals, clinics, and equipment. Modern facilities equipped with state-of-the-art technology can improve the quality of care and reduce waiting times.

Recommendation: Public-Private Partnerships

Collaborations between the public and private sectors can accelerate infrastructure development. These partnerships can share the financial burden and expertise required to create world-class healthcare facilities.

4. Enhancing Sanitation and Hygiene

Solution: Stringent Regulations and Monitoring

To address sanitation and hygiene concerns, healthcare facilities must adhere to stringent regulations. Regular monitoring and inspections should be conducted to ensure compliance and maintain high standards of cleanliness.

Recommendation: Training and Education

Proper training and education of healthcare staff regarding sanitation and hygiene protocols are crucial. Creating a culture of cleanliness and hygiene within healthcare facilities can significantly reduce the risk of infections.

5. Reducing Patient Waiting Times

Solution: Efficient Scheduling and Workflow

Healthcare institutions can optimize their scheduling and workflow processes to reduce patient waiting times. Implementing technology for appointment booking and tracking can help streamline operations.

Recommendation: Resource Allocation

Allocate resources effectively by assessing patient needs and staffing accordingly. This may involve cross-training staff to perform multiple roles and employing predictive analytics to forecast patient demand.

6. Ensuring Safety and Preventing Violence

Solution: Security Measures

Implement comprehensive security measures in healthcare facilities to ensure the safety of both patients and healthcare workers. This includes the presence of trained security personnel, surveillance systems, and controlled access.

Recommendation: Conflict Resolution Training

Healthcare staff should undergo conflict resolution training to de-escalate tense situations. Additionally, public awareness campaigns can emphasize the importance of treating healthcare professionals with respect.

7. Strengthening Legal and Regulatory Frameworks

Solution: Transparent Reporting

Enhance transparency in reporting medical errors and adverse events. A clear reporting system encourages accountability and enables institutions to learn from mistakes.

Recommendation: Mediation and Arbitration

Establish mediation and arbitration mechanisms to resolve disputes without resorting to lengthy and costly legal battles. These alternative dispute resolution methods can lead to quicker resolutions.

8. Addressing Ethical Dilemmas

Solution: Ethical Committees

Every healthcare institution should have an ethics committee to address complex moral issues. These committees can provide guidance on ethical decision-making in challenging situations.

Recommendation: Ongoing Ethics Education

Offer continuous ethics education to healthcare professionals to help them navigate complex moral terrain. Training programs can equip them with the tools to make ethically sound choices.

9. Supporting Mental Health and Well-being

Solution: Mental Health Services

Healthcare institutions should prioritize mental health services for their staff. Providing access to counseling and support can help mitigate burnout and stress.

Recommendation: Work-Life Balance

Promote work-life balance through flexible schedules and adequate time off. Encourage a culture of self-care and resilience within the healthcare workforce.

10. Preparing for Public Health Crises

Solution: Pandemic Preparedness Plans

Develop robust pandemic preparedness plans that include early detection, rapid response, and effective vaccine distribution strategies. Learn from the lessons of past pandemics to enhance readiness.

Recommendation: International Collaboration

Collaborate with other nations and international organizations to ensure a coordinated global response to public health crises. Sharing information and resources can help control the spread of diseases.

11. Balancing Healthcare Costs

Solution: Value-Based Care

Transition to a value-based care model that focuses on patient outcomes rather than the volume of services provided. This can reduce costs by eliminating unnecessary procedures and tests.

Recommendation: Price Transparency

Increase price transparency in healthcare by disclosing costs upfront. Patients should be aware of the financial implications of their treatment decisions, allowing them to make informed choices.

12. Promoting Equitable Healthcare

Solution: Universal Healthcare

Work towards achieving universal healthcare coverage to eliminate disparities in access and reduce healthcare inequality. Ensure that all citizens have access to essential healthcare services.

Recommendation: Health Equity Initiatives

Implement targeted health equity initiatives to address disparities in marginalized communities. These programs should aim to improve healthcare access, education, and outcomes.

13. Reducing Unnecessary Surgeries and Tests

Solution: Evidence-Based Medicine

Promote evidence-based medicine to guide treatment decisions. Physicians should base their recommendations on scientific evidence rather than financial incentives.

Recommendation: Second Opinions

Encourage patients to seek second opinions before undergoing surgeries or extensive medical tests. This can help identify unnecessary procedures and prevent harm.

Conclusion

The challenges facing the medical field are complex and multifaceted. However, with proactive solutions and thoughtful recommendations, it is possible to address these issues and create a more resilient and efficient healthcare system. Collaboration among healthcare professionals, policymakers, and the public is essential to implement these solutions effectively. By taking decisive action, we can ensure that the medical field continues to evolve and provide high-quality care to all individuals, regardless of their circumstances.

Introduction

The future of healthcare is a topic of immense importance, particularly in light of the myriad challenges faced by the medical field today. As we navigate the complexities of the evolving healthcare landscape, it is essential to consider the potential advancements and changes that could alleviate some of these challenges. In this chapter, we delve into the exciting possibilities and transformative innovations that hold the promise of revolutionizing healthcare as we know it.

The Intersection of Technology and Medicine

One of the most significant drivers of change in healthcare is the integration of advanced technologies. From artificial intelligence (AI) and machine learning to telemedicine and wearable health devices, the medical field is on the cusp of a technological revolution.

1. AI and Machine Learning in Healthcare

Artificial intelligence and machine learning have the potential to transform diagnostics, treatment planning, and patient care. Machine learning algorithms can analyze vast amounts of patient data to identify trends, predict disease progression, and even recommend personalized treatment plans. This not only enhances the accuracy of medical diagnoses but also improves patient outcomes by tailoring treatments to individual needs.

Moreover, AI-powered robotic surgical systems are becoming more commonplace, enabling surgeons to perform complex procedures with enhanced precision. These technologies reduce the risk of human error and minimize invasiveness, resulting in shorter recovery times and improved patient experiences.

2. Telemedicine and Remote Monitoring

The COVID-19 pandemic accelerated the adoption of telemedicine, allowing patients to receive medical consultations and follow-ups from the safety and comfort of their homes. This trend is likely to persist, offering increased accessibility to healthcare, particularly for those in remote or underserved areas.

Remote monitoring devices, such as wearable fitness trackers and home-based medical sensors, are also contributing to proactive healthcare management. These devices can track vital signs, detect early warning signs of illnesses, and provide healthcare providers with real-time data, enabling timely interventions and reducing the burden on hospitals.

3. Precision Medicine and Genomics

Advances in genomics (study of an organism's complete set of genes) are ushering in an era of precision medicine, where treatments are tailored to an individual's genetic makeup. This approach promises to improve treatment efficacy while minimizing side effects. Genetic testing can identify a person's predisposition to certain diseases, allowing for early intervention and prevention strategies.

The integration of genetic information with electronic health records (EHRs) enables healthcare providers to make data-driven decisions about treatment plans, medications, and preventive measures. This not only improves patient care but also enhances our understanding of the genetic basis of diseases.

Addressing Workforce Shortages

One of the pressing challenges in healthcare is the shortage of skilled professionals. This shortage extends across various healthcare disciplines, from physicians and nurses to radiologists and laboratory technicians. To address this issue, several innovations and changes are on the horizon.

1. Telehealth and Telemedicine

Telehealth and telemedicine not only improve patient access to care but also expand the reach of healthcare professionals. Through telemedicine, specialists can provide consultations to patients in remote areas, bridging the gap between demand and supply. Additionally, telehealth allows retired or semi-retired healthcare professionals to continue offering their expertise, helping mitigate workforce shortages.

2. Advanced Training and Simulation

Innovative training methods, such as virtual reality (VR) and augmented reality (AR), are revolutionizing healthcare education. Medical students and professionals can engage in realistic simulations, enhancing their skills and knowledge without putting patients at risk. These technologies also facilitate continuous learning and upskilling for healthcare workers.

3. Task Shifting and Nurse Practitioners

To address physician shortages, healthcare systems are increasingly relying on nurse practitioners and physician assistants to provide primary care services. These highly trained professionals can perform many of the tasks traditionally reserved for physicians, thereby expanding the capacity of healthcare teams.

4. Global Workforce Mobility

Globalization has opened up opportunities for healthcare professionals to work internationally. Cross-border collaborations and partnerships can help redistribute the healthcare workforce more evenly, ensuring that underserved regions have access to competent medical personnel.

Improving Access to Healthcare

Access to healthcare remains a global concern, with disparities in healthcare access and inequality persisting. However, innovative approaches are emerging to bridge these gaps.

1. Community Health Workers

Community health workers play a vital role in reaching underserved populations. These individuals, often from the communities they serve, provide education, preventive care, and assistance with navigating the healthcare system. By training and employing more community health workers, we can improve healthcare access for marginalized communities.

2. Mobile Clinics and Outreach Programs

Mobile healthcare units and outreach programs are bringing medical services directly to remote and underserved areas.

These initiatives offer vaccinations, screenings, and basic medical care, reducing barriers to accessing healthcare.

3. Digital Health Records and Telemedicine

Digital health records and telemedicine platforms are making it easier for patients to connect with healthcare providers. These technologies enable virtual consultations, prescription refills, and the tracking of health data, empowering individuals to take charge of their health.

4. Healthcare Financing Models

Innovative financing models, such as microinsurance and community-based funding, are being explored to make healthcare more affordable and accessible in low-income regions. These models aim to reduce the financial burden on patients and ensure that no one is denied care due to cost.

The Future of Medical Infrastructure

The state of medical infrastructure, including hospitals, clinics, and equipment, significantly impacts the quality of healthcare. To address the inadequacies in this area, several transformative changes are on the horizon.

1. Modular Healthcare Facilities

Modular healthcare facilities are designed to be scalable and adaptable to changing healthcare needs. These facilities can be rapidly deployed during emergencies or in underserved areas, ensuring that critical healthcare services are accessible when and where they are needed.

2. Remote Monitoring and Telemedicine Facilities

As telemedicine continues to grow, specialized facilities equipped with advanced telemedicine technology will become more prevalent. These facilities will provide a dedicated space for remote consultations and medical procedures, ensuring that patients receive high-quality care even from a distance.

3. Smart Hospitals

The concept of smart hospitals involves the integration of cutting-edge technologies to enhance patient care, streamline operations, and improve efficiency. These hospitals will feature AI-driven diagnostics, IoT-connected devices, and automated processes, reducing human error and optimizing resource utilization.

4. 3D Printing and Medical Equipment Innovation

3D printing technology has already revolutionized the production of medical implants and prosthetics. Prosthetics are artificial devices or replacements designed to replace or enhance the function of missing or impaired body parts, such as limbs, hands, feet, or other organs, helping individuals with physical disabilities to regain mobility and functionality. In the future, 3D printing technology may also enable the on-site manufacturing of medical equipment and even organs for transplantation, reducing the reliance on centralized manufacturing and distribution.

5. Telehealth for Rehabilitation

Telehealth is not limited to primary care; it can also be applied to rehabilitation services. Patients recovering from surgeries or injuries can receive physical therapy and rehabilitation guidance through telehealth platforms, reducing the need for in-person visits and increasing accessibility.

The Critical Role of Sanitation and Hygiene

Maintaining proper sanitation and hygiene in healthcare facilities is essential for preventing infections and promoting patient safety. Addressing this critical issue requires a multi-faceted approach.

1. Advanced Sanitation Technologies

Innovative sanitation technologies, such as automated disinfection systems and UV-C sterilization devices, are being developed to enhance the cleanliness of healthcare environments. These technologies can significantly reduce the risk of healthcare-associated infections.

2. Infection Control Training

Education and training programs focused on infection control and hygiene practices are vital for healthcare professionals. These programs ensure that healthcare workers are well-equipped to prevent the spread of infections within healthcare settings.

3. Patient Education

Patients also play a crucial role in maintaining hygiene standards. Providing patients with education on hand hygiene, proper disposal of medical waste, and infection prevention measures can contribute to a safer healthcare environment.

Reducing Patient Waiting Times

Excessive waiting times for medical care can have adverse effects on patient outcomes and satisfaction. The future of healthcare aims to address this challenge through various means.

1. Appointment Scheduling Algorithms

Advanced algorithms and scheduling software can optimize appointment bookings, reducing wait times and ensuring that patients receive care promptly. These systems can also account for the urgency and severity of a patient's condition, prioritizing those in critical need.

2. Teletriage and Virtual Waiting Rooms

Teletriage is the remote assessment and prioritization of patients' medical needs using telecommunications technology to determine appropriate care and referrals. Virtual waiting rooms are digital platforms or online spaces where individuals wait for their scheduled appointments or services, often in telehealth or online service settings, allowing for efficient and organized management of patient or customer flow.

Teletriage services allow patients to receive initial assessments and medical advice remotely, helping determine the urgency of their healthcare needs. Virtual waiting rooms enable patients to wait for their appointments from the comfort of their homes, minimizing time spent in crowded waiting areas.

3. Streamlined Administrative Processes

Efficiency in administrative processes can also contribute to reduced waiting times. Electronic health records (EHRs) and digital paperwork systems can eliminate bureaucratic delays, allowing healthcare providers to focus on patient care.

Safety and Violence Prevention

Safety concerns and incidents of violence against medical professionals are distressing challenges in healthcare. Addressing these issues requires a multi-pronged approach.

1. Security Measures

Hospitals and healthcare facilities are investing in security measures such as surveillance systems, access control, and security personnel to protect both patients and healthcare workers. These measures aim to deter violence and provide a safe environment for all.

2. Conflict Resolution Training

Healthcare professionals are increasingly receiving training in conflict resolution and de-escalation techniques. These skills help defuse tense situations and reduce the risk of violence in healthcare settings.

3. Community Engagement

Engaging with local communities and raising awareness about the importance of respecting healthcare workers can contribute to a more respectful and supportive environment for medical professionals.

Legal and Regulatory Frameworks

Navigating the complex legal and regulatory landscape in healthcare is a perpetual challenge. Addressing this issue requires ongoing reforms and innovative approaches.

1. Digital Health Regulations

As digital health technologies proliferate, regulators are developing frameworks to ensure patient privacy, data security, and the effectiveness of telehealth services. These regulations aim to balance innovation with patient protection.

2. Malpractice and Liability Reform

Malpractice claims can place a significant burden on healthcare providers. Efforts to reform malpractice laws and promote alternative dispute resolution mechanisms can reduce legal complexities and enhance patient-provider relationships.

3. Regulatory Compliance Solutions

Innovative solutions, including AI-driven compliance monitoring tools, can help healthcare organizations stay up-to-date with changing regulations and streamline compliance efforts.

Ethical Dilemmas in Healthcare

Navigating complex moral terrain in healthcare is an ongoing challenge. The future of healthcare will involve continued discussions and ethical frameworks to address these dilemmas.

1. End-of-Life Care

Advancements in medical technology raise questions about the ethics of prolonging life when there is no chance of recovery. Ethical guidelines and patient-centric decision-making processes are crucial to addressing end-of-life care dilemmas.

2. Research Ethics

In the pursuit of medical advancements, researchers must adhere to ethical standards and prioritize the welfare of study participants. Transparent and rigorous ethical review processes are essential for maintaining public trust in medical research.

Mental Health and Well-being of Healthcare Workers

Burnout, stress, and mental health issues among healthcare workers are significant challenges that require attention and support.

1. Mental Health Services

Healthcare organizations are increasingly recognizing the importance of providing mental health services and resources for their employees. Employee assistance programs, counseling services, and peer support groups can help address burnout and stress.

2. Work-Life Balance

Efforts to improve work-life balance for healthcare professionals can reduce burnout. Implementing flexible scheduling, providing opportunities for rest and recuperation, and ensuring reasonable work hours are essential steps.

Public Health Crises

The COVID-19 pandemic highlighted the need for robust preparedness and response strategies for public health crises. Lessons learned from this global event will shape the future of healthcare.

1. Pandemic Preparedness

Governments and healthcare organizations are investing in pandemic preparedness plans, including stockpiling essential medical supplies, developing rapid diagnostic tests, and establishing communication protocols.

2. Vaccine Distribution and Production

Efforts to improve vaccine distribution infrastructure and expand vaccine production capabilities are critical for responding effectively to future pandemics.

Healthcare Costs

The escalating costs of healthcare are a significant challenge worldwide. The future of healthcare must find ways to balance quality and affordability.

1. Value-Based Care Models

Value-based care models focus on delivering high-quality care while controlling costs. These models incentivize healthcare providers to prioritize preventive care and reduce unnecessary procedures.

2. Transparency in Pricing

Greater transparency in healthcare pricing can empower patients to make informed decisions about their care and put pressure on healthcare providers to offer competitive pricing.

Private vs. Government Healthcare

The debate between private and government healthcare systems continues. Understanding the differences and challenges is crucial for shaping the future of healthcare.

1. Access and Quality

Private healthcare systems often provide faster access to care, while government systems aim to provide universal coverage. Striking a balance between accessibility and quality of care is essential.

2. Funding and Resources

Government healthcare systems rely on public funding, while private systems depend on insurance and out-of-pocket payments. Finding sustainable funding models that ensure equitable access to healthcare is a complex challenge.

Unnecessary Surgeries and Excessive Medical Testing

Instances of unnecessary surgeries and excessive medical testing for financial gain are serious concerns in healthcare.

1. Evidence-Based Medicine

Promoting evidence-based medicine and clinical guidelines can help reduce unnecessary procedures. Healthcare providers should prioritize treatments and interventions with proven effectiveness.

2. Ethical Oversight

Ethical oversight committees and regulatory bodies play a critical role in monitoring and preventing unnecessary surgeries and tests. Strengthening these oversight mechanisms can safeguard patient interests.

Solutions and Recommendations

The future of healthcare is brimming with promise, but it also demands concerted efforts to address the challenges that persist. To navigate this future successfully, we offer practical solutions and recommendations.

Invest in Telehealth Infrastructure: Expand telehealth infrastructure to improve access to healthcare, especially in underserved areas. Ensure that patients have access to affordable internet services to facilitate telemedicine consultations.

Promote Interdisciplinary Collaboration: Foster collaboration among healthcare professionals from different disciplines to provide holistic and patient-centered care. Encourage team-based approaches to address complex medical cases.

Embrace Preventive Healthcare: Invest in preventive healthcare programs and public health campaigns to reduce the burden of preventable diseases. Educate the public about the importance of healthy lifestyles and regular check-ups.

Enhance Healthcare Education: Modernize healthcare education to incorporate emerging technologies, telemedicine, and ethical considerations. Provide ongoing training to keep healthcare professionals updated with the latest advancements.

Support Mental Health and Well-being: Prioritize the mental health and well-being of healthcare workers through comprehensive support programs, including counseling services, stress management, and work-life balance initiatives.

Strengthen Regulatory Oversight: Ensure robust regulatory oversight to prevent unnecessary medical procedures, protect patient rights, and maintain ethical standards in research and clinical practice.

Promote Transparency in Healthcare Costs: Advocate for transparency in healthcare pricing and billing. Implement regulations that require healthcare providers to disclose pricing information and offer clear explanations of medical bills.

Expand Access to Healthcare in Underserved Areas: Develop and implement policies that incentivize healthcare professionals to work in rural and underserved areas. Support community health worker programs and mobile clinics to reach remote populations.

Invest in Medical Infrastructure: Modernize healthcare infrastructure by adopting smart hospital technologies, modular facilities, and innovative sanitation solutions.

Prioritize investments in medical equipment and telehealth facilities.

Conclusion

The future of healthcare holds immense promise, fueled by the convergence of cutting-edge technologies, innovative approaches to workforce shortages, improved access to care, and a renewed focus on patient well-being. As we confront the complex challenges outlined in this chapter, it is evident that the medical field is evolving at a remarkable pace. The advancements discussed here, from AI-powered diagnostics to telemedicine expansion, represent just a fraction of the transformative changes on the horizon. By embracing these advancements, prioritizing ethical considerations, and implementing practical solutions, we can strive towards a future where healthcare is not only more accessible and efficient but also characterized by a higher quality of care, improved patient experiences, and greater overall well-being for both patients and healthcare professionals. It is through these collective efforts that we can shape a brighter and more resilient healthcare landscape for generations to come.

"Challenges and Solutions in the Medical Field" delves deep into the multifaceted landscape of healthcare, offering a comprehensive examination of the pressing issues that define the modern medical field. With a keen focus on both the challenges and potential solutions, this book explores the evolving nature of medical challenges in a world of scientific advancement, technological integration, and shifting demographics.

From the critical role of nursing and administration to the shortage of skilled professionals, inadequate infrastructure, sanitation concerns, and ethical dilemmas, each chapter dissects a crucial aspect of healthcare, shedding light on the complexities within. This book also draws invaluable lessons from the COVID-19 pandemic and navigates the intricate web of legal, regulatory, and ethical frameworks governing the field. It culminates in a visionary exploration of the future of healthcare, offering hope and insights for a brighter, more accessible, and ethically sound medical landscape.

ABOUT THE AUTHOR

Mr. C. P. Kumar is a retired Scientist 'G' from National Institute of Hydrology, Roorkee, Uttarakhand, India. He is also a Reiki Healer and Chakra Balancing practitioner (with pendulum dowsing) and offers Emotional Freedom Technique (EFT) to help individuals with emotional issues. Mr. Kumar has authored many books on technical, spiritual, and social topics.

For further details, you may visit his webpage
https://www.angelfire.com/nh/cpkumar/virgo.html

www.ingramcontent.com/pod-product-compliance
Lightning Source LLC
Chambersburg PA
CBHW071604270726
48661CB00018B/1150